VIDEO
FAMILY
HISTORY

VIDEO FAMILY HISTORY

by Duane and Pat Sturm

P.O. Box 476
Salt Lake City, UT 84110
801-531-1790

Library of Congress Cataloging-in-Publication Data

Sturm, Duane
    Video family history / by Duane and Pat Sturm
          p.   cm.
    Includes index.
    ISBN 0-916489-44-2 : $9.95
    1.   Video recordings--Production and direction--Amateurs' manuals.
    2. Video tape recorders and recording--Amateurs' manuals.
    3. Family--Folklore--Documentation--Handbooks, manuals, etc.
    4. United States--Genealogy--Handbooks, manuals, etc. I. Sturm, Pat
    II. Title.
PN1992.94.s78   1989
791.43'0232--dc19   88-35025
                                             CIP

Robert J. Welsh, Managing Editor
Design and Production by Robert Passaro

First Printing 1989
10 9 8 7 6 5 4 3 2 1

Printed in the United States of America

Contents

Illustrations

*This book is
dedicated to the 705 Crew*

O.M. Sturm

Ada Sturm

Mary Jane Sturm

Mary Lee Carey

Doug Sturm

Debra Sturm

and

Robert Spence

*without whose support
this book would not
have been possible.*

Additional thanks to

Alexa Keihl-Valles, our editor and friend,

*for her superb editing skills and warm personal support
throughout the development of this book.*

Introduction

It was just a little over a year ago that my dear Aunt Mary Jane first spoke with us about producing a video documenting our family history. Mary Jane's parents, my paternal grandparents, had passed on a few years earlier, and she wanted to record the family history of their generation and generations past before it faded from memory.

Mary Jane came to us because we had established Prismatic Productions, a small format video production company, a couple of years before. Using VHS video equipment, Prismatic Production's main business centered on videotaping weddings, reunions, and other such gatherings, but we also traveled to Nicaragua in 1986 and brought back enough tape to produce three documentaries on conditions in that proud but struggling country.

We jumped into the family video project with relish, rounding up old family photographs and other memorabilia, and planning a live family shoot for January, 1987.

The live shoot was a great success, producing about three hours of tape for us to edit, in addition to both old and new photographs. By the time we held the family premiere in May, the production had grown into what one local newspaper called, "a video epic," covering six generations, beginning with the American Civil War. In addition to the lengthy live segments recording the memories of Mary Jane and her five siblings, it contains over 340 photographs and other artifacts.

At the premiere and each subsequent showing of "The Life and Family of Clark and Hanna Sturm," the most frequently asked question has been, "Will you be making family history videos for other families?" We explained that, while most video projects are time consuming, an undertaking of this nature can be especially challenging. When discussing with a friend how a family video of this sort is really a labor of love, he suggested that the perfect solution would be for us to write a how-to manual with which to help home video enthusiasts produce their own family video.

With the advancements of video technology now available, nearly any family can, with a minimum of equipment and the special training this book provides, produce a family video that far surpasses the usual 8mm and Super 8mm home movies. The object of this handbook is to substitute ingenuity and elbow grease for fancy equipment and expensive studio fees. All of the techniques described within are designed for consumer video equipment operated by family members. While we have employed these methods primarily with the VHS format, the general techniques outlined here can also be applied to other video formats, such as Beta and 8mm video. There are also several examples of props and video tools that your crew can make which require few special skills to construct. Our desire is to offer a variety of ideas and options from which the home producer can choose to produce his or her own unique video.

Producing a family history video really *is* a labor of love, and it is also a perfect family project, with each member happy to be part of a video production crew. As a team, the family is drawn closer together while they work to learn about their roots. Each member can share the achievement of recording his or her family history in this exceptionally creative way.

This book explains in simple, matter-of-fact terms, how to produce the highest quality video that home equipment allows. It also offers many tips to make your production as interesting and entertaining as possible.

Primarily, the method used to accomplish this production is to combine as many audio and visual sources as possible. For example, the visual aspect can include elements from one or more of the following: photographs, both old and new; graphics, like family trees and maps that you make yourself; the best parts of those old home movies; slides; and live video segments. For the sound track, a creative producer can mix written narration, music, and the recorded voices of any number of family members. All of these different audiovisual sources are blended like the fine ingredients of a favorite family recipe to create a production guaranteed to become a treasured heirloom. Each chapter contains a list of options, leaving you, as the home producer, free to choose exactly which approach is best suited to your family. One of the easiest videos to produce is one which combines a series of photos and other still visual material with a sound track of narration and background music. On the other end of the production spectrum is a family video that begins with photos and other visuals but also includes segments of a live shoot. Whichever approach you choose, every production method stresses the highest possible quality within the boundaries of consumer video standards. As a home producer, you will also find that many of the techniques and methods described by this book can be used in other types of home video productions.

There are several good video books and magazines on the market that you are advised to read and study. One that we have found particularly useful, *Single-camera Video Production*, by Barry J. Fuller and associates, has been consulted in the preparation of this handbook. However useful such books can be, we have found that the most valuable teacher is usually experience itself. At best, books and manuals can only offer techniques and methods that must be modified to fit each individual's needs and desires.

We recommend that you read this book in its entirety before deciding what kind of family video you wish to produce. There are many questions to consider, but the most important prerequisites for your project are desire, time, and patience.

As you read through the first time, make notes of the ideas you would like to use in your production. Then, next to each idea, list the type and amount of material and equipment needed to transform each idea into becoming a part of your video.

Try to estimate the number of hours each step will require and multiply the total hours by two to find the time the entire project will take. Divide the total hours by the number of family members on the production crew to make sure everyone is willing and able to invest the amount of time such a project requires.

We have tried to avoid using too much video jargon, but at times it is impossible to write about the subject without using the special vocabulary it has created. When you are unsure about a term, please refer to the glossary in the back of this book. Sometimes our video term usage may not be exactly the same as that of the video industry, but in such cases we have tried to shape the language so that it can best be understood by the home video enthusiast. The illustrations will also help elucidate these terms and concepts.

It is our fond desire that families everywhere will use the methods detailed in this book to produce family genealogical videos that will be cherished and treasured for years to come. Everyone shares those rare photos and stories of people and places past, which together form the collective memory of the family. Even more than a pictorial and oral history, this video becomes a memorial to the generations upon which every family is built. To know from where we come permits us to know ourselves that much better. And future generations may be given the chance to know those things about ourselves and about our ancestors that are too easily lost in the winds of time.

Duane and Pat Sturm
December, 1987
Georgetown, Florida

CHAPTER ONE

Thinking It Through: A Creative Overview

Why Produce a Family Video ? 1.1

Although at first glance this question may appear to have a simple answer, there are actually several reasons why you may want to make a professional looking video about your family. It is very important to have a concrete answer to this question of "why," because it will shape the entire concept and, in turn, the finished product.

The first step in producing a family video is to list the reasons for your wanting to do it. While some of these reasons are mentioned in the introduction, such as recording your family's roots and providing a project the whole family can work on together, there are many more. Perhaps you want to create a video tribute to grandparents who have passed away in order for your children, and their children, to remember them better. Possibly there are some very special family members, like Great-Uncle Henry, who are getting on in years, and you want to record their memories before it becomes impossible. It may be that several family members have different photographs that you would love to collect and assemble into a pictorial history to record on video. You may want to produce a family video for a special upcoming family event, like a reunion or fiftieth wedding anniversary. Sometimes families share a special interest or hobby, anything from auto racing to bird watching, and that can be the primary focus of the video.

The reasons you want to produce a family video might include several of the above possibilities, and as you list them (one of the many lists demanded by this project), determine which ones are the most important to you. Number them in order of priority but remain flexible for new ideas which may arise and need to find their proper place in the production. Always remember that the suggestions listed above, like all of those contained in this book, by no means exhaust the possibilities of ideas which can be used in your production. Your effort should reflect the uniqueness of your family; as no two genealogies are the same, no two family videos will tell the same story.

1.2 The Next Important Questions

Who Can?

Although video has now been around for several years, it is still very common to find people who regard it as belonging in the company of astrophysics or some other pursuit beyond the limitations of the average person. Nothing need be further from the truth. Today's home video equipment is designed to be easy to use, so no one should believe that mastering the video techniques outlined in this book are beyond his or her capabilities. There are really only two basic requirements for learning how to produce simple videos: desire; and the time to study the methods.

Of Whom?

The strength of a video production is usually dictated by the strength of the theme. This is especially true for a family video production. One of the most common mistakes is a storyline that meanders from subject to subject without apparent direction.

There are a number of possible treatments for the family history video. Perhaps the most favored is a straight-line, chronological progression from the earliest known ancestors, through each succeeding generation, to the present family members. This type of treatment can be focused still more sharply by using as the central subject(s) a family leader or particular "primary" couple. For example, the family video we produced about my father's family told the story of the clan through the lives of my grandparents. Remember, the primary subjects need not necessarily be living; in the above example they were not. Such a focus also becomes a kind of tribute to loved ones lost and an ideal vehicle for introducing them to generations too young to have known them personally.

One of the beautiful aspects of a family video is its ability to unite the family's efforts on a single project, so as many members must be included as possible. You should, however, be aware that it becomes easy to spread the focus too thin by trying to concentrate in-depth on too many people. This is especially true in large families, so you will have to decide where to draw the line when including in-laws, cousins, and other more distant relatives. Be sensitive and uniform in your decisions, remembering that you have a maximum time limit of two hours per videotape. Although this may seem like plenty of time, we can assure you that it is eaten up very quickly when people start reminiscing over old photographs. Review the section1.1, "Why Produce a Family Video?" and make a list of the reasons you want to produce a family video. Talking it over with your family, number in order of importance, from the strongest to the weakest, the focuses you wish to have.

Who Can Help?

The answer to this question is easy . . . *everyone!* Make sure that you make the production of your video into a family project. Everyone will enjoy watching it so much more if they also had a hand in making it, and there are tasks which family members of every age can help perform. Although you will not need all of the following jobs filled in every family video production, at least some will be important to each one. In addition to a camera person, editor, and director, you may also need to use able and talented relatives in the roles of carpenter, researcher, calligrapher, musician, lighting director, property recorder, graphic artist, audio technician, and last, but certainly not least, writer. All of these crew members can also have assistants to help them. There can be a part in the production for every member of the family, and all of these production workers' contributions should be noted in the production credits which conclude the video.

1.3 Developing the Concept

There are three major stages required to produce any video program. The important first stage is developing the concept. This is the thinking part, the task of organizing everything in your mind and on paper before you ever pick up a video camera. The second stage uses the video camera to record current family members. Actually, a live shoot is not necessary to produce a perfectly satisfactory family video. In some cases, depending on the focus and the family, other visual materials such as photographs, slides, home movies, and a host of others, will not only be sufficient to show the story but are also the preferred method. The third stage, postproduction, involves all of the studio work: the visual transfers mentioned above, editing live shoots (if any), and recording the audio track of the production. This is the stage where the work is completed. Your studio can be any quiet room in the house, and you can work on postproduction at your convenience.

The type and amount of audio/video equipment that you have access to will also be a major influence on developing the concept of your family video. Chapter 2, "Preparing For Action: A Technical Overview," will describe what is possible and is not possible with the level of equipment described in this book.

One of the most important parts of producing a family video is developing the concept. After reading this manual you will have a clearer idea of the options available in producing it and can then define your particular family situation by listing the "whys" and "whos" discussed in sections 1.1 and 1.2.

To help with these listings you will need to research your family story. It is time to include others in the family; the kids become "investigative reporters," digging out those old photos and "interviewing" grandpa and grandma about *their* parents. Begin collecting the special photos and other artifacts that will be transferred to video. Be sure that *all* items collected are numbered and recorded by the "property recorder." We use those small, round self-adhesive labels to stick the numbers on the backs of the photos and other items. Remember, many of these things will be one-of-a-kind and priceless to the owners, so treat all items with the care and respect they deserve. Others will appreciate your attention, and it will add to the professional quality of your production. As more and more visuals are collected, they will slowly shape the story you will tell. Begin a rough outline that you can fill in as you gather new information. Be aware that each story will need visual material to illustrate it. If Uncle Jim has a great story about his African safari, you must make sure that he has enough photos and/or other visual material to show for the duration of his narrative.

Your family may be prompted to learn more about their past. There are many resources available to assist you in discovering details about your roots. Libraries with a genealogical collection are a great place to start. You will be able to learn the exact titles of published genealogies and how and where to obtain a copy. *The Source: A Guidebook of American Genealogy,* edited by Arlene Eakle and Johni Cerny (Ancestry, 1984), has been described as the best reference book in existence on genealogical records. It is available from Ancestry, Inc. Another useful reference book is the latest edition of *Genealogical and Local History Books in Print,* 4th edition, compiled by Netti Schreiner-Yantis (Genealogy Books in Print, 1985).

The largest collection of genealogical information in the world is housed by The Church of Jesus Christ of Latter-day Saints. For more information on their extensive genealogical resources you may write to Family History Library, Genealogical Department, Dept. P, 35 N. West Temple, Salt Lake City, UT 84150-0001.

You may find it helpful to contact the National Genealogical Society, Education Division, 4527 Seventeenth St. North, Arlington, VA 22207-2399. Send a stamped, self-addressed envelope, and they will send you a pamphlet, "Suggestions for Beginners in Genealogy."

During this time you want to be thinking about various family members' talents which may be enlisted in the production. As you refine your focus and begin to determine the type of family video you want to produce, it will also become apparent what kinds of jobs you need filled and which family members are best suited for them. Remain flexible about job responsibilities at this point, not forgetting that some members of the video crew are able to perform a variety of functions. Keep in mind that producing a family video can be a deeply fulfilling communications exercise for the entire family. Conduct meetings at convenient times to discuss every aspect of the project. Invite other relatives who have expressed an interest, keeping to an agenda or outline at the meetings in order for all members to get a feeling of discipline and organization. A professional atmosphere makes the project more fun and meaningful, and easier in the long run for all.

Before the meetings, have the family read all or parts of this manual so they have a better idea of the range of possibilities. Encourage them to use their imagination to come up with ideas about how best to produce a video about the family.

Gauge the response of your family to the idea of making the video. A lot of work is needed for such a project, and if interest is lacking at the beginning it means more work for those really involved. When checking the general enthusiasm remember, everyone finds it much easier to pitch in if they are given specific assignments to perform. It is your responsibility to create the circumstances which best promote everyone's involvement in the project.

One of the most important decisions to be made at these "concept" meetings is whether or not the family video will include a live shoot. Let's go over the pros and cons of a live video shoot.

One problem with editing live material into your production is that it will require the additional equipment mentioned in section 2.1; another VCR and TV or monitor. It also requires that the producer or editor learn how to edit using two VCRs, as explained in section 4.6, "Video and Audio Editing."

The live shoot or shoots require a considerable amount of work and organization on the part of the crew and family in order to be a success. A few more crew members are needed, and, not least of all, there must be willing cooperation from those being recorded.

However, after mentioning this, there is still no doubt that a live shoot adds a very special dimension to the production of your video. Family members are preserved on tape "in action," to be remembered just the way they are. Who can explain old photos better than the ones who experienced those times? Stories that you have enjoyed again and again take on new life when they form the narration as photos appear, like magic, on the TV screen.

Live segments also make the final production more interesting; the program cuts back and forth from still visuals to live action. The audio track from the live shoot can be edited in with photos and other visual items to avoid long stretches of "talking heads." A live shoot provides more audiovisual options with the final editing (see audio editing in glossary) and lends a warm personal touch to the production that nothing else matches. It also provides an opportunity for bringing the extended family together. With recording sessions which include three or four relatives at a time, you can capture spontaneous interactions that the family will treasure for years to come. Later generations will be able to glimpse recent ancestors whom they could never meet personally.

Chapter 3 explains in greater detail how to get ready for a live video shoot. But before you start planning, make the suggested lists and carefully consider the pros and cons of a live shoot. Meet with the crew after everyone has read section 3.1 concerning essential equipment and what it takes to have a good live shoot. Compare opinions about the necessity and feasibility of including a live shoot in your production plans. Remember, you can produce a very good video about the clan without the addition of a live shoot.

If the consensus is to include the shoot, you should still list any and all anticipated limitations which may hinder the project. These include any of the areas referred to in the first three sections: lack of proper equipment, or funds to rent them; a strict budget in relationship to other costs both large and small; restrictions on the available time of crew members; any other limitations particular to your situation. Try to be as realistic as possible and imagine every possible pitfall. When you have decided what your course will be, it is time to prepare for either a live shoot, or, if you have decided not to include a live shoot, to move on to postproduction.

CHAPTER TWO

Preparing for Action: A Technical Overview

Getting Started: Essential Equipment 2.1

A while ago we received this self-described "pearl" from a seasoned producer, "You must understand the capabilities and deficiencies of your equipment *before* you decide what to do with that equipment." While this is certainly true, it has been our experience that more often than not, it is the potential of the audio/video equipment that goes untested and the imagination and zeal which are lacking. For example, anyone with a video camera or camcorder and a tripod can incorporate still photographs and other flat art in his or her footage. But how often is this done? The same can be said regarding the inadequate attention given to the audio track in most home enthusiast recordings. We therefore tend to stress utilizing the full capabilities of the audio/video equipment which many families already have rather than focus on possible deficiencies. In general, you might be surprised at the number of creative touches you can employ without adding to the basic equipment list found below. By basic we mean those items necessary for a pictorial production consisting of a series of photographs with a narration and background music. The list includes the following:

1. A video camera
2. A tripod for the camera
3. A VCR with an AUDIO DUB feature (if you are using a camcorder check it for that feature)
4. A TV or video monitor
5. An audiocassette tape recorder with either an internal or external microphone (external is preferred for "cleaner" recordings)
6. A phonograph (or additional cassette player)
7. A stopwatch
8. A bright light
9. A simple graphics board that you can make yourself (see illustration 10 on page 55)

And that's it! Many of these items can be found in your home. With a couple of exceptions, the equipment necessary to create your own video can be rented. While the majority of those wishing to produce a family video will probably already have their own video camera and VCR, it is not an absolute necessity.

To produce a family video that includes both photographs and live shoot segments, you will need two more pieces of equipment. In addition to those listed above you will need another VCR and another TV. These are needed so that you can perform some rudimentary editing, combining segments of still visuals with videotaped portions of a live shoot.

Maybe you would like to add the best parts of those old 8mm and Super 8mm home movies. The only additional equipment is the proper film projector and screen. And how those silent movies come alive when you add some sound, be it narration, music, or both!

Or perhaps there are some special times, maybe a trip or vacation, which mean a lot to your family, but have been almost forgotten because they were recorded on 35mm slides that now sit in boxes in the basement. Again, all that is needed to include them in your family video is a slide projector and screen. Once transferred to videotape the slides look much like photographs on the TV screen.

The only other piece of equipment of any importance is an audio mixer. This nifty little unit allows the operator to combine audio signals from at least two different sources, for example, instrumental music from a record and narration recorded on cassette tape, can be "mixed" and sent to a VCR where they are recorded together as the sound track of your family video. Radio Shack markets a few different models, one for under $100. The one we use is the Realistic "Stereo Mixing Console."

However, even this modest investment in an audio mixer is not essential to production. The instrumental background music behind the narration can be recorded on the cassette tape simply by playing it low while recording the voice. A few experiments are required to determine volume levels. Although, this is a trickier technique than using a mixer, because the narrator must be more careful not to make a mistake and so require starting over. But all of this will be explained in much greater detail in section 4.1, "A Creative Audio Track."

Although these artistic touches will make your production more professional in appearance, you cannot produce a truly professional video using consumer video equipment. Do not expect results of TV network caliber from half inch video formats. VHS, and the other half inch formats to a lesser or greater extent, lose a substantial amount of picture clarity, or resolution, each time a copy is made. If you shoot some raw footage, edit that tape onto a master tape, and then make copies of the master, those copies are two generations from the raw footage. Depending on the quality of the tape and equipment used, the amount of lighting, and other factors, copies can lose 30 percent or more of the original resolution.

There are numerous tips contained in this book designed to keep generational resolution loss to a minimum; their importance cannot be overstated, so we will briefly mention a few important points in this chapter.

Take the time to familiarize yourself with the general conditions under which video equipment produces the finest footage. While video cameras, for example, do best with bright light, they cannot tolerate the contrast of brightly lit areas and regions of shadow or darkness. Conversely, a poorly lit setting which produces a grainy result is made even worse by the glare the camera produces when it pans across a source of light such as a window, an open door, or an indoor light bulb.

The white balance feature on your video camera or camcorder tells the camera how to "see" true color by using white as a reference. To white balance, focus the camera at any white surface using the same light under which you are going to record, and activate the white balance set switch for a few seconds. Proper use of the white balance and light is your best guarantee of recording "true color." If your white balance has an INDOOR/OUTDOOR setting, make sure you use it. Experiment with your camera's white balance in relationship to various lighting conditions until you thoroughly understand how to obtain the best possible picture quality under all circumstances. It is a good practice to think through a shot before you start the camera, critiquing the camera movement and setting the proper focus for your final destination. Try not to rely on the "automatic" mode of the white balance and camera focus; you can usually do a better job after you have refined your technique with a preliminary run or two through each shot. This applies both to flat art and live subjects, although in "real shoot" situations flat art is much easier because live subjects often move and speak too quickly for the camera person to manage a practice take. When you review the recorded footage, write down notes that indicate areas in which the camera technique might be improved, and how.

Use your tripod as often as possible. Smooth camera movement enhances any live shoot and is essential when the camera lens zooms in on flat art. The tiniest shake or shiver is noticeable whenever the camera is on a closeup shot.

Try to use a fluid head when recording the flat art and photos particularly; it really makes a difference. If you cannot obtain a fluid head for the flat work and find it difficult to perform smooth camera movements, it is best to keep such movements to a minimum. Sometimes it can be just as effective to cut to different parts of one still photograph (provided it's large enough), using the in-camera editing techniques introduced later in this section.

Another area of video production that many home enthusiasts do not take full advantage of is the audio track. Again, the deficiencies are usually not with the equipment. The microphone which is provided with the camera and a tape deck with a microphone and a turntable/amplifier combination is all that is needed to produce an interesting audio track for your family video and any other productions. The addition of a directional microphone which plugs into your VCR or tape deck is an inexpensive way to improve noticeably your audio recordings, but it is not an essential piece of equipment. The same can be said about an audio mixer, graphic equalizers, and other audio shapers.

Fundamental Editing Techniques 2.2

The two main types of video editing described in this book are in-camera and on-line. The easiest is in-camera, so named because the ON/OFF trigger of the camera is used to establish the cuts between different shots. This method works perfectly for the portions of the family story that can be told with a collection of photographs and other flat art.

Numerous possibilities are listed in section 4.2, "Visual Transfer Candidates." For photographs and flat art the producer needs the following essential equipment: a video camera and VCR *or* a camcorder; a tripod with a good quality head; a graphics board or easel to hold the flat work; and a bright light, preferably of the same kelvin temperature with which your camera functions best. While section 4.3 gives a complete explanation of in-camera editing techniques, the method it speaks of relies chiefly on using the mounted camera to record a series of photographs and flat work. Each item is assigned a certain time span on the screen, depending on the length of narration that will be added onto the audio track. To add the audio track requires a VCR or camcorder with an AUDIO DUB feature, and a cassette tape deck equipped with either an internal microphone or, better yet, an external microphone on a cord.

In-camera editing is the least time consuming method of production of your family history on video because it eliminates the challenge of connecting a series of live segments into a cohesive narrative. Family members can collect the needed materials, writing the narration to fit the visuals. The narration is recorded on cassette tape and then timed to determine the number of seconds each piece of flat work will be on the screen. Add a little background music at the beginning and end, and the result is a professional looking family history on video.

The other primary method of editing video is on-line, which means editing between one or two slave VCR(s) and a master VCR. This is the method you will use if you want to include live segments in your family video. Live subject matter is almost always too difficult to edit using the in-camera technique because there will be footage which you will want to exclude from the master, or edited tape.

As mentioned earlier, with on-line editing you will need at least two VCRs (or one VCR and a camcorder) and two TVs or monitors. It is also very helpful to have an inexpensive switcher, SEG, or enhancer of some sort, although it need not be considered essential equipment. As with in-camera editing, if you want to record narration, background music, or both on the audio track, you will need a VCR or camcorder with an AUDIO DUB feature. Various combinations of on-line video and audio editing are described at length in section 4.6.

All of these combinations of editing techniques are achieved by connecting specific pieces of audio/video equipment with patch cords. The patch cords are plugged into the equipment jacks that route the signal flow from one piece of equipment to another. In this way the signal can be first shaped by enhancers, proc amps, switchers, and SEGs, and then recorded on the video track of a VCR. Audio signals are shaped by amplifiers, graphic equalizers, and audio mixers. They are usually recorded on cassette audio tape, or, for a video program, on the audio track(s) of the master videotape. Patch cords make all of this possible. They come in all lengths and with a multitude of plugs and jacks, so the first step in connecting your equipment is to determine how the audio/video signals can best be routed through to your recording equipment. Write down the type of jacks in your equipment that must be matched with the proper plugs. There are adaptors, if necessary, which change the size of some plugs. For a complete explanation of this subject, turn to the part in section 4.1 called, "A Word About Patch Cords, Y Cords, Jacks, and Plugs."

There are also several illustrations that should help you determine which patch cords and related hardware you will need to hook up your editing station. After you become experienced with editing audio and video segments at your station, you will see which aspects of your camera work can be improved and modified to add ease and smoothness to your on-line editing. You will also begin to identify breaks in the raw footage that provide the most convenient editing points, and you will realize the important role a live audio track plays in determining a good edit point. All of this will make you appreciate the value of connecting an audio mixer in the path of your audio signal, because you will then be able to control the volume level of the raw footage before it is recorded on the master. By quickly fading out the audio signal at the end of a sentence, the editor can more easily perform a pleasing visual cut away from the speaker.

As with most other pursuits, the amount of time invested by you and other family members improving your editing techniques will be directly proportional to the amount of skill you attain. Approach each editing session as an opportunity to refine your technique and add to your video "bag of tricks." You may feel that the progress is slow at first, but with practice you will proceed much more rapidly. Editing is a time consuming procedure, which is a good reason to know your own editing capabilities and time restrictions before deciding on the size of your family video.

The solution to the time consumption issue is to enlist the help of as many other family members as possible into the editing process. For example, various editing responsibilities include one or more technician(s) who are in charge of signal routing, patch cords, and the general functioning of the editing system(s). There may also be more than one editor and assistant editor for such specialized work as shooting flat art and audio editing. The editing team is supported in their work by writers, collectors, graphic and background artists, and assistants. The more responsibilities that are divided among family members the less time any particular individual will need to invest in the project. Try to tailor the range and scope of your family video to fit both the size of the production crew and the type and amount of audio/visual equipment you will be using. Exactly how much time a certain element of the production will consume is nearly impossible to calculate, because there are countless variables. Those closest to the project are the only ones who are able to estimate how much time any certain procedure will require. Constant communication between members of the crew is necessary to insure that one or more of the team does not become overburdened with responsibilities.

CHAPTER THREE

Action!
A Live Shoot

Getting Ready for the Live Shoot 3.1

The Family Becomes the Crew

The crew for the live shoot must consist of at least three members, but not usually more than six or seven. All crew members should be familiar with the concept and focus of the production and have read as much of this book as possible. They should also know fully what their tasks and responsibilities are *before* the day of the shoot.

The location of the shoot must afford two separate and distinct areas: a waiting room, and the actual site of the shoot, either indoors or out. A minimum of two crew members are needed at the shoot site, the camera person and the floor manager. In the waiting room one crew member can record, or log, photos and visual items, and also advise those to be videotaped, but it is much better if there is at least one crew member for each job. In fact, preparing the people for the camera by forming them into groups and arranging the photos which will be used, is a task of great importance and can be handled by several crew members. Those who can instill confidence in the talent and calm them are highly valued. The photo recorder's job in the waiting room is also indispensable because in postproduction the editor will only be able to match the proper picture with the correct story if the waiting room record is accurate. It is also the record used to return the photos and other items to their proper owners. At the site of the shoot the camera person is in charge of the proper use of all equipment. An assistant standing by can be of great help, especially when unexpected events arise.

The floor manager's task is to introduce those being videotaped to the recording operation, explaining the need for the bright lights (the best resolution for the recording), telling them to speak one at a time and as distinctly as possible, and various other tips necessary to produce a quality video. For example, if the camera operator finds, through the viewfinder of the camera, that there is a glare on someone's nose, the floor manager will be asked to move the person to another chair or apply a little makeup to the offending area. As with crew members in the waiting room, the floor manager's primary responsibility is to insure the talent's greatest comfort, keeping them as relaxed and natural as possible in a situation which is new and uncomfortable.

The Talent

Determine the most convenient place and time to conduct the live shoot. Indoor shoot sites are favored because the circumstances can be controlled, and they are not subject to the adverse weather conditions which can play havoc with an outdoor shoot. Bright sunshine is not the best source of light for a video shoot because it creates great contrast of light and shadow, something that video cameras cannot manage well. It is important that the shoot site be very quiet to obt<in as "clean" an audio recording as possible, so here again, indoors is preferred.

When you have decided on a good location and time, send a letter to all potential participants, including in it the general concept and format you are considering for the video. Explain that every member of the family who would like to help may, either in the production of the program or as talent in front of the camera. Set the date far enough in advance to let everyone reserve that day on their calendars, making it clear who is invited to be recorded. This list of talent can be modified, but it should be established to give a certain structure to the shoot. In a week or two, follow up the letter with phone calls to get some direct feedback. Keep a record of the responses from different family members. Ask for independent ideas and suggestions and assure participants that nothing is unchangeable within the production. After gauging the response, perhaps an adjustment to the overall plan will need to be made. Enlist support for the project from the leadership of the family; this will encourage participation from all members. Younger generations of the family can help the elderly remember favorite family memories. One method to control the number of talent, particularly if you have a large family, is to limit on camera performances to siblings and their spouses of a certain generation, and perhaps their parents. Include as many subjects as possible while retaining the desired focus.

The Equipment

Before deciding to include segments of a live shoot in your family video, assemble an editing station using as a minimum two TVs and two VCRs connected with patch cords. Since editing is a postproduction function, there is a thorough explanation about how to edit in section 4.6, "Video and Audio Editing." There is no reason to have a live shoot if you are unhappy with your attempts to edit using this rudimentary technique. Practice with some video you have already recorded, follow the instructions in section 4.6 carefully and exercise as much patience as possible.

One way to practice editing is to make a "preparation" video to show and/or send to members of the family. Include examples of old photos transferred to video and also live segments of you explaining your ideas for the family video production. Made with a sense of humor and imagination, this introduction to the project can propel the family into action by giving a hint of just what can be done to produce an interesting video.

There is another editing option. Take your tapes to a video studio and either have the work done for you or rent time and do it yourself. This type of studio can be found at some universities and in larger cities. However, there are a few drawbacks to this method. The cost of the production immediately rises; studio time, especially with an operator, is expensive. Another problem is that you will probably want to cut back and forth from live to still visuals, and this can only be done if: (1) you have already shot all of the photographs and other visuals on a separate videotape, or (2) you also rent a graphics video camera shooting your still visuals in between your live segments as you edit there in the studio. With the first choice you lose a generation before your still visuals are on the master tape with a corresponding loss of picture resolution. This is true not so much with the master tape, but with the copies made from the master. Picture deterioration when copying is always present in the half-inch video formats, both VHS and Beta, regardless of the quality of the equipment used to record and transfer the material. Remember, in VHS production you may lose up to 30 percent or more of the picture resolution of the master, depending on how many generations there are between the original raw footage and the final copies. To compensate for this loss we stress methods which are designed to produce the highest quality production available using half-inch equipment. This includes the highest quality tape on the market, the fastest recording speed (SP), and shooting all still visuals directly onto the master tape.

If you are considering the second option of shooting stills in between live segments, consider it almost a necessity to hire operators for the studio work. Although the results of this technique should be a high quality program, the production costs will be equally high. The main purpose of this book is to show you how to produce a high caliber family video without needing to use a professional studio. With the studio method there is also a danger that the personal touch you would want with a family video production might be lost.

When you are satisfied with your editing decisions begin arranging for the live shoot. Prepare a sheet of "organizational notes" outlining important information to be remembered during the shoot.

On the day of the live shoot the two primary activities are videotaping family members in the shoot room and collecting and organizing visual materials (photographs, slides, home movies, memorabilia, etc.) in the waiting room. All conversation recorded on tape during the live shoot should pertain to specific visual material, because the finished production will feature a combination of both. Your "organizational notes" should look something like this:

1. The shoot room;
    a. It is important to eliminate noise, both in and outside of the shoot room, for a high quality audio. Have only one person speak at a time while taping.
    b. Use bright lights to obtain the finest picture quality possible.
    c. Powder faces to eliminate shine when filming.
2. The waiting room;
    a. Organize visual materials by topic.
    b. Identify all visual material on the back with: the owner's name, the names of people and places in the photo, and the date the photo was taken.

    c. Label each piece of visual material with an identification number and list the number in a log.

    d. Place all visual material items in the appropriate collection boxes, organized by topic.

    e. Emphasize to the family that all stories recorded on videotape will need visual material to present with them. Help each person to be videotaped choose photos and other visual material that will illustrate the spoken memories. Talent may bring these materials into the shoot room and use them when they are videotaped. These audiovisual relationships should be recorded by the camera person or his/her assistant on a separate log to be used by the editors in postproduction.

    f. Answer any questions, working to calm and instill confidence in any members nervous about the recording experience. Help them polish their delivery, rehearsing with them what they intend to say.

    g. Collect one or two sentence self descriptions from all participants and any important dates or events that will help the writer(s) with the narration. Coordinate members into groups in such a way that will encourage memories of special events and eras. Welcome and record all ideas.

    h. Deposit visual items in the proper collection box when finished.

Xerox these organizational notes and give a copy to each crew member at the live shoot. Next, assemble the equipment and materials to be used at the live shoot.

The Shoot Room Preparation

Naturally you will need a video camera and VCR or camcorder. We advise you to clean your camera lens. In addition, check your VCR to see if the VCR heads should be cleaned. We recommend using the "wet-type" head cleaner about once every two months, depending on how much you use the machine. Plenty of videotape is essential. It's best to use EHG or professional tape.

You should concentrate on two other areas of video technique for a quality shoot production. The first is effective lighting. Basically, you must flood the area where the talent will sit with light. Although video cameras are capable of adjusting their color picture according to the amount of "hot" light (regular incandescent bulbs) or "cold" light (florescent) they encounter, the best color is obtained by using lighting with the kelvin temperature (K) for which your camera is designed. There is a range of kelvin temperatures, but most are around 3200 degrees K. To use this type of lighting you can buy "photo flood" bulbs at any good camera store. They are around 300 watts, approximately three to four dollars each, and a set usually requires two to four of them. These bulbs burn very hot, so be careful with them. You will also need light fixtures to put your photo floods to work. We have found that painter's scoop lights, those with shiny metal hoods shaped like a fat bell, with a heavy clip that allows it to grab on to a variety of objects, work very well. These feature a ball joint which lets the fixture turn in almost any direction. Be careful in handling the paint scoop lights immediately after they have been used. They become very hot due to the photo flood bulb, so let them cool down after use.

Check the electrical circuit being used for the shoot. While the camera and VCR draw comparatively little power, the lights, especially as more are added, may use a great deal. Inspect extension cords and fixtures before and during operation to insure proper safety. (If cords become too hot to hold, unplug them.) If you detect a buildup of heat in any cords or equipment, stop the session and allow everything to cool. Split the electrical load onto different circuits whenever possible.

Reflectors are useful at the shoot. They can be as simple as 3' X 3' sheets of cardboard painted white or covered in aluminum foil (shiny side out). Placed in strategic locations they bounce light from the sources onto the subject. While they are not mandatory, they can be used to rid unwanted glare or light up a dark corner of the frame.

The other area of video technique requiring attention at the live shoot is the audio track. Audio quality is as important as good lighting or camera technique. The most significant problem with regard to audio recording is the placement of the microphone, or mike. Video cameras are equipped with a mike that is usually located somewhere near the lens drum. These mikes are omnidirectional, meaning they record sound that comes from all directions. This works well when the camera is positioned very close to the subject being recorded but quickly becomes unsatisfactory as the distance between them increases. One way to alleviate this problem is to obtain or make a mike cord which places the mike in close proximity to the subjects, while at the same time it is plugged into the camera across the room. Check to see if your camera mike detaches from the camera. If so, find a mike cord of the proper length and with the proper plug and jack. (For more about this subject see the discussion in section 4.1, "A Word About Patch Cords, etc.") If not, check the manual to determine if the camera has separate jacks on it, making it possible to connect another external mike (many have this feature). Such a microphone can be purchased for as little as twenty dollars, a wise investment that can be used repeatedly to produce superior audio for your video. Remember to check the pickup pattern of the mike; it ranges from narrow (unidirectional) to wide (omnidirectional). For a family shoot a wide range is best unless you want the subjects to move in front of the mike before they speak, or to pass the mike. The first is a rather awkward technique, and the latter is strongly discouraged because it encourages audio "bumps" and "rattles" which ruin

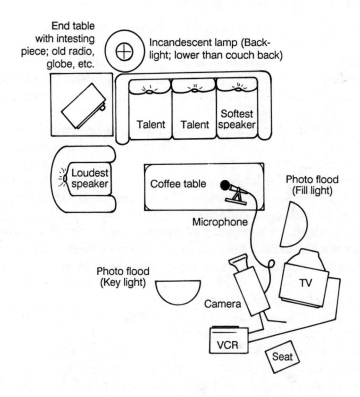

Illustration 1: Bird's-eye view of a shoot room

your original intention: to obtain clean audio. Make sure you use a mike cord that is long enough and is shielded from outside interference.

To make the set look more natural camouflage the mike by placing it in an arrangement of silk or dried flowers placed on a coffee table directly in front of the speakers. Test your audio connections before recording "for real." A small change in the position or direction of the mike can sometimes make a sizable difference in its performance. Sit people with soft voices closest to the mike and those booming speakers farthest away (see illustration 1).

The Waiting Room Preparation

You will need a number of cardboard boxes in the waiting room to collect and separate the visual materials (mainly photos, slides, memorabilia, etc.). Clearly label each box according to topic or family, but also label boxes for special shared topics, i.e., World War II, the Depression, a fiftieth wedding anniversary.

Record what goes into the boxes by designing record sheets which will enable you to keep the visual materials organized. Label each item with an identification number; we use self-adhesive labels, placing them inconspicuously on the back of the visual materials. The record sheets should correspond with each collection box topic. Record the number which identifies each item of visual material for that topic. Leave a half to full page under each topic heading for the identification numbers. (Some topics may have twenty to forty items, for example.) While it is unnecessary for the identification numbers to be in numerical sequence, make sure that all items have a separate, unduplicated number. Two different items with the same number could cause confusion.

When each visual material item is labeled with an identification number and the number is written down on the record sheet under the appropriate topic heading, place the visual in the correct collection box.

Orderly record sheets are very important because they enable the production crew to know at a glance the topics which are lacking visual material. This information is also vital for the writers because they must fill in visual "holes" with materials found elsewhere, such as those listed in section 4.2, "Visual Transfer Candidates."

3.2 The Day of the Shoot

The crew should get to the location of the shoot early to prepare the waiting room and the actual shoot room. In fact, we recommend an allowance of at least a couple of hours to prepare both the waiting and shoot rooms, with enough time remaining for a last short meeting before the talent arrive.

At this meeting give each crew member a copy of the "organizational notes" that were previously discussed. Explain the notes point by point, answer any questions, make sure that each member understands his or her responsibilities for the day, and thank everyone for their help and participation.

The Waiting Room

Choose a large room or rooms (a garage works fine) for the waiting room which is far enough away from the shoot room so that absolutely no sound from the waiting room can be picked up on the video recording. Have plenty of chairs, a few tables, some refreshments, and enough comforts to soothe nervous subjects. Arrange the boldly labeled collection boxes so that they are easily accessible.

As the family members being videotaped arrive, they should be briefed by the producer and crew about the general recording operation. When everyone is present, assemble the crew and talent together for a pep talk, and review the "organizational notes." It is unnecessary for the talent to have a copy because the crew will be assisting them with each step of the process. Thank everyone for their cooperation and let them know which crew members will assist the talent in the waiting room.

After family members have been formed into talent groups and have chosen the pictures they wish to talk about, sample questions may be offered in the waiting room to initiate conversation with each other in front of the camera. Any questions should pertain directly to the visual materials. Here are a few examples:

1. Tell us about the people and/or place in this photo.
2. When and why was this picture taken?
3. What was happening in this picture?

4. What do you remember about the special event
   in this photo?

Remember, these are only general prompters to encourage spontaneity and natural conversation. If these questions are taken into the shoot room, warn the talent that loose
papers can create unwanted noise on the audio track.

Perhaps a word should be mentioned about having
children as talent in the live shoot. While it is entirely possible
to include children "on camera," it is much easier to have their
parents or other, older relatives talk about them. Then, in the
editing process, the childrens' pictures can be used to illustrate
the audio. However, this is one of those many areas in this type
of video production where the producer must decide how best
to tell the family story. One factor that should be considered
is the number of youngsters in the family and their ages. In
truth, many children become extremely self-conscious and shy
when the camera is on them and usually contribute little.

If you want to include children with some live segments
consider recording them while they are engaged in an activity
they enjoy. This requires organizing several special shoots or
using videotape recorded at some other time by the different
parents. It is difficult to give every subject consistent treatment
when you expand the live shoot to include children.

When in doubt about what to record on the day of the
shoot, go ahead and film everything as long as time or electrical power is not a problem. Later, in the editing process, you
can determine what footage to include in the master. One nice
feature of video as compared to film is that the editing process
in video does not in any way mar or destroy the original (or
raw) tape from the live shoot.

The Shoot Room

Choose a large, comfortable, quiet room. Use as background
to the talent one wall which is a solid color, preferably a light,
pastel or neutral shade, without windows or mirrors. If you
must use a wall with a window, close the curtains to eliminate

any unwanted reflections. Arrange the seating by forming an "L" with a sofa and large easy chair. (see illustration 1, page 25) Position the camera so it is pointed into the corner of the "L," which will allow it to pan easily to all subjects. You can use a small table with an antique radio or similar bric-a-brac to fill in the void. Place a coffee table to shape a disjointed triangle with the "L" formed by the chair and sofa.

For lighting, collect ordinary paint scoop fixtures and load them with the proper photo flood bulbs. One easy way to put the fixtures at the proper height is to mount them with spring clamps atop long-backed chairs, positioned in such a way that the lights form a rough triangle, as shown in illustration 1 (see page 25). It often works best to have one light, usually the key, higher than the others. For this use a stepladder or something similar, making sure that the light clamp is on the ladder securely and will not slip.

Once your lights are in place use three or four members of your crew as practice talent to adjust the direction of the lights. Have them sit where the talent will be and fine tune the positions of the lights. Your goal with positioning the lights is to reduce all remaining shadows.

Standard three-point lighting calls for a key light, a fill light, and a back light. Two of your photo floods can serve as the key lights, providing the main illumination. Position your remaining photo flood, the fill light, opposite the key lights to eliminate the strong shadows they cast. As you refine your lighting scheme, remember to place a short table lamp behind the sofa to act as a back light. This is important because it adds "depth" to the set and creates a much more pleasing picture. As you experiment with the placement of the back light, make sure that the fixture is not seen by the camera. Try different watt bulbs in the back light; three-way lamps are easy to adjust. Using a regular incandescent bulb in the back light is acceptable because it has a tendency to add additional "red" light to the set and create a "warm" texture to the video picture. Check your completed lighting setup by shooting a little tape with your practice subjects and examining the playback. One way to check your lighting while adjusting it is to connect a TV or monitor to your VCR or camcorder auxiliary unit.

For the camera setup, mount the camera on the best tripod you can obtain. If you do not already have a tripod, remember that the head is the most important part when you rent, buy, or borrow one. A tripod with a "fluid head" as opposed to the spring-loaded type is best because it has a far smoother motion. With the camera on the tripod, go through camera movements with your practice talent in order to see what focusing and other adjustments will be necessary during the shoot. We recommend leaving the camera on manual focus if possible, because a camera operator with a good eye can usually produce a sharper focus than most consumer cameras on automatic focus. With all of the camera work remember that the bottom line is to do whatever will result in the highest quality recording.

We also prefer manual white balancing over the automatic method. Let the camera warm up for ten minutes before manually white balancing, using the lighting on the set. This will produce the best color of which the camera is capable. Here again, having the camera connected to a TV or monitor lets the camera operator immediately evaluate the picture the camera is producing.

Before shooting, the camera operator should prepare the high quality videotape being used by fast forwarding it to the end and then rewinding it to adjust it to the VCR being used. Each tape should be adjusted in this manner and also numbered for the shoot log.

Review a final test recording to assure your satisfaction with the practice set conditions. Watch and listen for flaws in the test recording. Is there any shake in the picture when the camera moves from one subject to another? If so, check the tightening screws and try weighting the tripod with sturdy plastic bags filled with sand or pebbles around its feet to help stabilize it. If there are any points of glare or distraction in the set remove or cover them.

Is the audio loud enough to hear each practice talent well? Are there any outside, unwanted noises on the audio track? Eliminate the sources of any undesirable noise. Disconnect nearby phones and consider unplugging the refrigerator; it will make more noise than you think. Post a reminder on appropriate doors that "shooting is in progress." Careful preparation will pay off in higher quality results, so spend the time to do the most thoughtful job possible.

Be extremely careful to avoid pointing any video camera without a lens cap at any bright light, such as the photo flood bulbs or the sun. Doing so can cause "burn-in," which leaves a permanent flaw on any future video recorded with that camera.

If the mike on your camera cannot be moved to the table, and the unit has no provision to plug another external mike into it, you must use the mike attached to the camera. In this case, move the camera, tripod, etc., as close as possible to the talent but make sure that you can zoom back wide enough to capture all of the subjects at one time. This is called an "establishing shot" and is used to introduce the viewer to the entire scene before zooming in on separate subjects. Set the camera level at the height of the subjects' eyes when they are seated. This is the most flattering angle for the subjects and also allows the viewer an intimate, eye-to-eye, encounter.

If possible, power the camera and VCR on household current, 110 AC, because it is the most reliable. If you use batteries make sure they are freshly charged and watch their condition throughout the shoot. Batteries seem to have a knack for going dead just as some beautiful, one-of-a-kind event begins to unfold.

Even the most expensive video cameras usually cannot tolerate areas of heavy contrast between light and shadow. Make sure that every inch of your set is flooded with as much light as possible. Even cameras that boast a low-light capability perform much better when used with plenty of light. The superior resolution this provides becomes very important in the editing process and in making final copies, which will by then be two generations removed from the original live shoot footage.

If your camera has the ability to create internal titles, you may want to consider adding this to your live shoot. This operation can be tricky to put into action, because once the shoot gets under way the camera person has many other details to occupy his or her thoughts. You might want to try it, though, at least during the practice session, so you can see how it works. These are decisions to be discussed with the crew. They are of special interest to the editors, since they must incorporate all such effects into the final production.

Consult the equipment manuals during the setup of the equipment. With the manuals, this book, and experimentation you should be able to achieve an operation which will produce pleasing results. The talent, after an hour or so of preparation in the waiting room, can now come in and tell their stories. You are now ready to begin.

The Shoot

During the shoot it is important to remember that regardless of how technically prepared you are, it is the mood and attitude of the talent which will determine the real success of this portion of your family video. Those speaking are the stars and should be made to feel that way, so do everything possible to help them feel comfortable in the shoot room. One way is by having the crew relaxed and informative. Casually point out the mike hidden in the flowers with a joke about being "bugged."

Keep in mind the audio/video transitions connecting each shot while using the video camera. Most of the time this is a straight cut from shot to shot, but even here the camera person must be careful to leave an extra couple of seconds *after* the last words of each shot are spoken, or the words will be cut off by the back-roll of the next shot.

Because you leave the camera rolling most of the time at the live shoot, transitions at the beginning of each segment are important. The fade up, either automatic or manual, is most common, but another transition is to defocus. With this transition the camera lens is intentionally turned to defocus, or blur, the subject. While the camera is rolling, the camera operator smoothly and quickly brings the subject into focus. Both the fade and defocus transitions, used to mark the end of a particular segment, should serve definite purposes at each use. Used haphazardly or too often, they soon become tiresome.

When the floor manager has everyone seated and settled, turn the camera on and ask the talent in what order they will speak. Keep the angle wide to include all of the subjects, then zoom in on the one who will speak first, and set your focus.

After a few minutes rewind the tape and, on a monitor the talent can view from their seats, play back what you just shot. This has three benefits. First, the talent receive some instant gratification by seeing how they look on TV, and it is usually much better than anticipated. This can have the effect of helping them relax and achieve that quality of being natural. Second, it allows the camera operator to make a final check of the quality of the audio and video, and third, you are now pre-focused and ready to start the shoot. Do not erase this practice segment by shooting over it; just get ready to shoot again.

The floor manager should powder noses for glare and remind everyone not to knock against the coffee table or drum nervous fingers. Explain that this is to keep the audio track as clean as possible.

Set your camera on a good establishing frame: wide enough to include all who are in the scene, but as close as possible to aid in clear identification and recognition. With a prearranged hand signal to the talent, begin recording with a fade up if your camera has this function. Immediately start a slow zoom in on the first speaker, having already pre-focused your camera for it. It is now mostly a matter of moving from speaker to speaker and avoiding excessive camera movement. Always shoot with an eye towards easy editing; it will save the nerves and sanity of the editors, and they will be forever grateful. The most uncomplicated and useful shot to edit in is a close up of whoever is speaking. If two people, sisters for example, are talking about a time or experience they have shared, widen the camera angle to include both of them. In this way, the camera will not have to jump back and forth as the subjects take turns speaking. Keep the camera zoomed in as close as possible, however, without cutting either out of the frame. Keep most of your footage on close-ups but remember to begin *each* session with a good establishing shot of the entire scene.

The camera operator and his or her assistant(s) are responsible for keeping a precise log which records the following:

1. Tape number
2. Talent names
3. Numbers of items talked about by a particular talent
4. Exact times of sessions
5. The number of "counts" recorded by the VCR tape counter in each session.

Take short breaks between sessions for everyone to catch their breath and make adjustments in the operation. During this time the producer should be the project's troubleshooter. This is done by gathering recommendations from every member of the crew for refining the system and improving the result. Strive to remain flexible during the shoot in order to take advantage of any new and creative opportunities that present themselves. Perhaps someone is unexpectedly able to attend on the day of the shoot; keep the shooting schedule flexible enough to include him or her. Or maybe once Grandpa starts talking about his boyhood in Iowa the session will grow longer than anticipated—but what priceless footage! Have plenty of tape ready and a full day's patience. The time you spend in detailed preparation will result in a live shoot which adds life, warmth, and humor to the finished production.

CHAPTER FOUR

After the Live Shoot: Postproduction

Overview

Postproduction refers to all of the audio and video editing that transforms the separate parts, audio track, live footage, and still visuals, into a unified and finished video production.

A Creative Audio Track 4.1

Producing a creative audio track may seem an odd place to begin your postproduction, but there is a good reason for beginning here. To a large extent the audio track will dictate the tone, content, and certainly the timing of your family video. If a live shoot is included in your production, you already have one recorded source for the audio track. But you will probably find that the talent has not told the entire story of the family and the holes must be filled in with narration. You may also use audio cassette recordings from relatives living elsewhere and/or parts of audio recordings made by family members from an occasion in the past. Just remember to have visuals which illustrate the audio recordings.

Establish a deadline for receiving both audio and visual material from family members. Once all of this raw material, including the live-shoot footage, is all together and scattered around your living room, your task is to review everything and organize and mold it into a comprehensible and focused format.

By this time you should have in mind which background music selections will best compliment the production. If there are any musicians in the family, perhaps they can contribute an original score or a couple of well placed songs. Try to think of any music that might have a special significance for events or people in the family's past. The visual material collected determines, in large part, how much freedom the writers have in creating the narration. If a substantial amount of narration is used consider having it read by more than one narrator. This can be especially effective. It adds an interesting touch to the narration if the speakers are of different sex and divide their parts according to the most appropriate gender.

It is the writers' responsibility to recognize areas that have visual material but lack an audio explanation. For each of these areas, the writers must write mini-scripts which connect the pieces of the story that already have both visuals and audio with the aforementioned ones. If you did not conduct a live shoot and are not using other audio sources, the narration tells the entire story.

The writers will probably wonder how long to make the narration or mini-scripts. While there is no absolute answer, a rule of thumb is that the still visuals, unless they are of extreme importance or special significance, should be on the TV screen an average of only seven to ten seconds each. So the writers should arrange, in logical order, the photos and other visual materials to be used for segments in need of narration, and multiply the number of items by eight seconds. This will provide a rough idea of the length the written script need be. Use this as only a general guideline, however, because there may be several times when one visual is left on the screen for twenty seconds or even more. There may also be several times in which the narrator pauses while the camera lingers on one or more visual(s). Thoughtful hesitations such as these are useful for setting the tempo of the production.

The producer and writers assemble the different parts of the entire production and write both the audio and video onto what is known in video production as a storyboard (see illustrations 2 and 3). The storyboard produces the program "on paper" so that every aspect of the production can be inspected and analyzed *before* it is committed to videotape. It shows at a glance where material is needed and when continuity breaks down between segments. Producing a clear storyboard is probably one of the most difficult, and one of the most important, tasks of the entire project. It is the blueprint from which the production is built, so take the time to refine your storyboard; make several drafts, revising it until you are satisfied. We cannot stress enough that the degree in which the final production "hangs together" will be due, in large part, to how well the storyboard is developed.

As parts of the storyboard are completed begin recording those parts of the written narration onto audiocassette tape. While it is possible to record the narration directly onto the videotape, we have found that it is easier for everyone to record the audio, whether it is narration or an original musical piece, on audiocassette first, and add it to the family video at your convenience.

When recording the narration the stress, once again, is on quality. It is most important to use the highest quality audio tape and equipment to which you have access. If possible, use a cassette tape recorder that accepts an external microphone, because they are superior to the internal type. You might be able to use the same mike that was used with your VCR during the live shoot.

Name: *Steven*	Project: *Family Video* Page *6* of *23*	
Video	**Time**	**Audio**
Cut to live segment of Uncle Gordon talking about his boyhood	0:00	"I was born in Herman, Minnesota in 1924. When I . . . ."
Fade up to photo #63 Gordon at age twelve. (11 seconds)	1:49	". . . . then at about age twelve . . . ."
Cut to photo #70 Gordon at age fifteen. (10 seconds)	2:00	". . . . worked in the fields with Dad and . . . ."
Cut to photo #65 (5 seconds and then slow zoom in to Gordon's face; total time: 20 seconds.)	2:10	". . . . when the war broke out . . . ."
Cut to photo #69 Gordon outside barracks Slow tilt up to camp sign. (20 seconds)	2:30	". . . . first sent to Camp Davis . . . ."
Cut to army medal: Purple Heart. Super close up (10 seconds)	2:50	". . . . it was in the Philippines that I was wounded by . . . ."
Cut to photo #73 Gordon arriving home (10 seconds)	3:00	". . . . and then I got shipped home . . . ."
	3:10	". . . . glad to be home."

Illustration 2: Written storyboard showing visual transitions

Name:	Project:	Page of
Video	**Time**	**Audio**

Illustration 3: Blank Storyboard

The narrators must become very familiar with the script. As they practice the narration, the audio technician, or the one most experienced with audio gear, can adjust the tape recorder. Make sure the bias selection matches the type of tape, and use any noise reduction system the machine has. If the recorder can record on metal tape, consider using this type for its higher reproduction properties. As with the live shoot, find a quiet place to record, unplugging any nearby refrigerators and other sources of unwanted noise. While the narrators speak check the VU meter, if the recorder is so equipped. The VU meter measures the volume of the audio signal. Most of the time the needle of the VU meter should register from -3 to 0, with peak loudness at $+1$ or $+2$. (0 equals the ideal level at 100 percent modulation.)

After recording a few takes of each piece of narration, number the tape and record its contents on a log sheet. On the log list the parts of narration recorded, the number of takes for each part, and the best take. Also include the exact length of each take that will be included on the video master. When you begin to add all of the pieces of audio in the editing process you will be glad to have such detailed logs on each tape. The part of section 4.6 entitled "Recording an Audio Track on Video with Prerecorded Visuals" discusses these methods.

We are describing audio techniques for VHS single audio track. If you are using Beta video equipment the task of producing an audio track is easier because Beta format has two audio tracks. If the audio channels on your Beta VCR have separate selection and volume controls, you can add the background music after the rest of the production is edited. This can be done without disturbing the narration and voices of the live shoot participants which have been recorded on one channel. This two-step approach is much simpler and results in a smoother production.

Much more could be said about audio techniques for video, but these basics should allow you to obtain audio recordings of ample quality for your family video. To learn more about this important aspect of video production there are several excellent books written on the subject you may wish to read. One that we recommend is *Audio in Media*, by Stanley R. Alten (Wadworth Publishing Company).

If other family members would like to contribute audio recordings for the video, instruct them on the basic techniques for making quality recordings. Perhaps, if they live nearby, you can arrange a session or two with them to insure that some quality accompanies the effort. Those residing further away can be mailed a list of audio recording techniques which we have just outlined. As a word of warning, it can be rather frustrating to try incorporating audio recordings of noticeably different qualities into a single audio track for your video production.

When you have collected and recorded the complete audio track for your family video, time it with the appropriate visual material. The easiest way to do this is to make a list of the key words on the audio track that signal a cut from one visual to the next. On the latest edition of your storyboard write the key words in the audio column and, directly across from them in the video column, the number you have assigned to the photo or other visual material (see illustration 2, page 38).

Begin the audio recording using a stopwatch or a watch with a second hand to time how long each visual will remain on the screen. This is the timing blueprint you will use for either in-camera or combination editing. For further details read section 4.6, "Video and Audio Editing," especially noting "Combination Editing."

In considering the use of background music for your video production, remember that it is one of the most effective tools available for adding continuity to different segments of any video program. Different methods can be employed to add background music to your production. The one you choose depends largely upon whether or not you are going to use an audio mixer. The audio mixer has one function: to receive audio signals from different sources and combine them into one output signal. This single output signal is then recorded as the audio track on your master videotape. The audio mixer is of utmost value for adding a professional touch to your video production, and there are audio mixers for under one hundred dollars from retail outlets such as Radio Shack. If you purchase only one piece of audio/video equipment to produce your family video, make it the audio mixer. Not only will it make the task of adding the audio track to your video production much easier, it will also give the most professional results.

The most rudimentary way to mix the narration and background music without an audio mixer is to have the background music playing softly while the narration is being recorded. Find the best volume for the music by making a few test takes. Fade the music slowly just before the narrator is finished with each segment. If you do not fade, the music will cut off abruptly when you add the audio in the editing, creating a disconcerting and unprofessional impression. Mark the position of the narrator and mike so that they are always in exactly the same place and have the music source turned to the same volume when recording each segment. Uniform sound is thus insured when the segments are joined together in the final production. Also, leave a few seconds of silence both at the beginning and end of each segment. This makes for smoother transitions when adding the segments together later.

Before discussing the next type of audio mixing, again without an audio mixer, we need to introduce patch cords and related equipment.

A Word About Patch Cords, Y Cords, Jacks, and Plugs

Many people think of concepts and terms derived from film with regard to video. But whereas film incorporates a *mechanical* process, projecting a strong direct light through moving celluloid pictures, video utilizes an *electronic* process, using a strong electromagnetic head to rearrange tiny metal-oxide particles bound to polyester tape. Once the particles are rearranged, or recorded, the tape reproduces the audio/visual signals when you press PLAY. These factors make videotape more like audiotape than film.

Because the VCR can send audio/video signals electronically, patch cords are used to route these signals to and from different pieces of equipment. Just as speaker cables connect your stereo to your speakers, so too can audio/video patch cords connect your stereo to a VCR. If the VCR has an AUDIO DUB feature, you can record a new video audio track from a vinyl record or cassette tape that you play on your stereo. One quick note: with or without an audio track the visuals must be recorded first. Also, be aware that using the AUDIO DUB on the VCR will completely erase the first audio track. However, this setup allows you to add your favorite music to some imaginative visuals and create your own music videos!

As you begin checking your equipment you will notice that there are many different kinds of jacks, those holes that audio/video plugs fit into, on different pieces of equipment. The most common kind of jack/plug combination with consumer video is the phono type (see illustration 4). However you will also find two other types of plugs and jacks quite often, the much larger earphone type, and the smaller mini-type used primarily for mikes. When you want to connect equipment you will have to determine which types of patch cords and ends are needed.

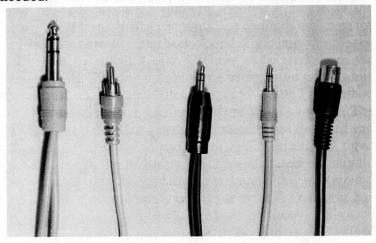

Illustration 4: Audiovisual plugs (left to right); 1/4", phono, mini (stereo), mini (mono), RF (radio frequency)

Patch cords come in a wide variety of lengths and with several types of plugs, but at times you will also need adaptors. These devices are used to change the plugs of your patch cords so that they fit into a certain type of jack. You will find that there are countless types of adaptors as you search for that elusive one you need.

Many pieces of equipment such as amplifiers, audio mixers, switchers, etc., will have stereo audio jacks. Unfortunately, the VHS video format has only one audio track and, therefore, only one audio input jack, often labeled MIC. Use double audio patch cords to connect gear when both are equipped with stereo jacks. Illustration 5 shows three types of Y cords that are very handy when you want to connect equipment with stereo jacks to equipment which has only one audio input, such as a VHS VCR. Be aware that when you use a Y cord the stereo audio signal changes to mono. If your master VCR does have stereo audio input jacks, use a stereo patch cord.

Be sure to distinguish between stereo and mono plugs and jacks, because both types are found on patch cords, Y cords, and adaptors. A mono plug has one black insulating strip around the lead, while a stereo plug has two black insulating

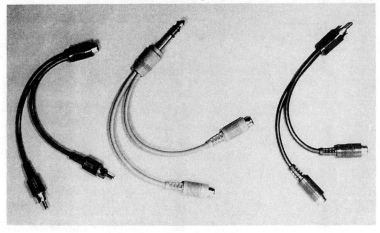

Illustration 5: Y cords

strips around the metal lead. Using a stereo plug in a mono jack, or vice versa, is not recommended, although it can be done in a pinch. You risk damaging both the jack and plug if they are not matched, because tiny electrical arcs jumping between unmatched leads can cause little pits in the metal itself. *Remember, always use the proper attenuator patch cord to protect the audio input jack of your VCR* (see page 62 for more on attenuators).

Aside from these cautions the video producer has an immense amount of freedom to record, via patch cords, a sound track collected from a variety of audio sources. It is almost impossible to damage equipment badly by hooking something up wrong; usually the only problem is that it does not work as it should.

Always remember the direction of the signal flow when you are using patch cords to connect different equipment. The audio or video signal, coming out of some source, can be routed through such shaping equipment as mixers and switchers. The signal continues until it reaches the input jacks of the master VCR, where it is recorded as the master audio track. This may sound complicated, but once you understand the fundamental requirements of any signal flow you will be able to hook up, and troubleshoot, the connections between almost any consumer audio/video equipment. Do not be afraid to try different hookups if you have an idea that demands the use of new equipment. Just remember that every piece of equipment adds a little more unwanted noise to the signal. You may want to take unnecessary equipment out of the signal flow to have the cleanest sound possible on your master video tape. Train your ear to catch the quality differences which exist between all audio sources.

Another source of unwanted noise when working with video, derives from the type of patch cords you use. The cable most familiar to consumers is the coaxial type. It is commonly used to bring the cable networks to the living room TV. Coaxial cable is a good medium for TV and radio transmissions because it can carry over a hundred different signals at one time. But for the same reason it is the least desirable cable to use with audio/video equipment because so many signals can "crosstalk" and create unwanted noise. Coaxial cables connect to radio frequency (RF) jacks on TVs and other equipment. Care should be taken not to bend or break the fine center wire at the ends of coaxial cables when connecting them to RF jacks.

Audio/video patch cords that carry one signal are much cleaner and therefore preferred. Get the best patch cords you can afford and take care not to bend them too sharply or let anything smash them. Most VCRs use phono plugs, except for those with a microphone jack, which often only accepts a miniplug.

With this information about patch cords, we can now discuss another way of mixing background music and narration. You can use background music from a record player or tape player that is connected to the master VCR with a patch cord. This is better than the previous method because patch cords provide a more controlled edit and are impervious to external noises, such as a knock at the door or a phone ringing. If you are going to have family members perform the background music it is easiest to make a good clean cassette tape recording of it which can then be patched in during the audio editing.

The music is mixed with the voice by using a Y cord. One leg of the Y is connected to the output of the cassette tape recorder that plays the previously recorded narration. The other leg of the Y is connected to either another audiocassette player or a phonograph which is playing the backgound music. The single leg of the Y is connected to the microphone jack of a VCR that is equipped with an AUDIO DUB feature (see illustration 6). The volume of both the narration and music is controlled by the volume knobs on the machines (either tape recorder or phonograph amplifier) that are being used as audio sources. Be sure to use an attenuator between the VCR and Y cord so that the VCR is not damaged by too strong of a signal from the machines feeding into it. Because it is difficult to monitor

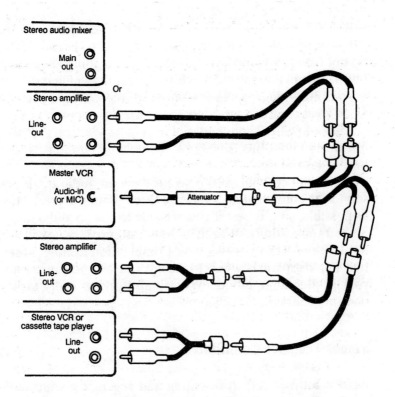

Illustration 6: Connecting one stereo audio source or audio mixer to a mono master VCR, or connecting two stereo audio sources to a mono master VCR.

accurately the proper volume levels of the two feed machines, trial and error are the surest ways to obtain the volume levels which sound the best. Also, try turning the bass very low while leaving the treble at about 60 percent. When you get the results you want, *make note of the exact positions of all volume controls* so you can duplicate your efforts every editing session. With patience and practice you should obtain results with which you are happy.

This same technique can be used when adding background music to the audio you want to use from the live shoot. Instead of a cassette tape recorder playing the narration into and through the Y cord, use a VCR playing the proper audio, along with the background music, on the other side of the Y. The problem with this Y cord setup is that most consumer VCRs do not have a volume control for the audio going either in or out of them. You must, therefore, adjust the volume of your narration coming from the cassette tape recorder to match the voice level recorded on videotape at the live shoot. If you are not including live shoot material in your production you need not worry about this; simply set the volume on the narration until it sounds right.

Remember, your goal is to produce an audio track that sounds as consistent and uniform throughout the production as possible, so it is best if you are able to use an audio mixer. Since its operation is utilized in the editing process we will wait until we reach the discussion of "Combination Editing" in section 4.6, to explain how best to incorporate an audio mixer into your production methods. We will also review audio techniques in general in that chapter.

4.2 Visual Transfer Candidates

Before getting too far in writing and organizing your audio track you might encounter situations where you will want to include audio that has little or no visuals. This can happen with audio both from the live shoot and narration. Instead of deciding to leave such stories out of the production, consider some visual candidates in addition to photographs, slides, and home movies. Some of these you can make yourself and others you can find elsewhere.

Some of the visual candidates can be found among the family heirlooms. Old obituaries are valuable as sources of information for writing the narration and also to be used sparingly as visual material. Old letters can be utilized in the same way, especially if they pertain to special moments in the family history. When letters are used as visual material, be sure to include close-ups of the envelopes if the address, stamp, and date of posting are at all clear. Printed invitations for marriages, birthdays, anniversaries, etc., can be very effective visual material if they are readable when transferred to the TV screen. They are especially beneficial as introductions to particular segments of the family video. Old newspaper articles are often interesting visual material, and even more so if they include a photograph. Try to include the date of the article in the picture or in the narration.

Other printed materials that look good on TV are special awards such as "Teacher of the Year," worker awards, diplomas, and certificates of accomplishment. Although not printed material, union buttons and military medals are often a colorful addition to the family production.

Other sources of visual material are pictures and illustrations found in books. While most of this material is copyrighted, it is usually not illegal to reproduce it if you do not intend to sell the reproduction commercially or charge admission to view it. These types of pictures can be very helpful if you need visual material from a historical era, such as the Civil War or the Depression. If you are concerned with the transferring, contact the Government Printing Office in Washington D.C., and ask for House Report #94-1476. It should answer any questions you may have about copyrighted material.

Another excellent way to establish time in your production is to use calendars from appropriate years. This visual is even more effective if the calendars were produced for a past or present family business and the name is prominently displayed. Business cards of different family members provide another good visual.

As you can see there are many more candidates to use as visual material for your family production than you may have first thought. No doubt there are many more than those included here and probably some that are especially suited to your production. If you need visuals which you just cannot seem to find, make them yourself. Here are some examples of possibilities, but the visuals needed for your unique produc-

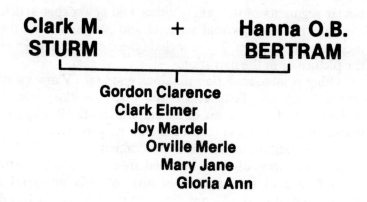

Clark M.   **+**   **Hanna O.B.**
STURM   **BERTRAM**

Gordon Clarence
Clark Elmer
Joy Mardel
Orville Merle
Mary Jane
Gloria Ann

Illustration 7: Example of a family tree

tion may not be included, so be creative and come up with your own ideas!

One of the most helpful visuals to explain your story is a family tree. A family video could include several different trees to illustrate the separate branches of the family, the historical progression, and so on (see illustration 7). Trees can be made by typesetting the information, or, more inexpensively, by handwriting it. Perhaps a member of the crew has a talent for calligraphy. Family trees are one of the best teaching tools to

Illustration 8: Example of a map

employ in your production, especially if they are combined with thoughtful narration.

Maps are another visual means of telling the family story. They should be simple (see illustration 8) and straightforward, with a minimum of words printed on them. A bold color scheme can also help, but do not make the maps too busy. Be sure you read section 4.3, "In-Camera Editing Techniques," before you spend a lot of time working on your visuals, because there are some additional tips to keep in mind to obtain the best results.

There are other visual materials of more limited use that you can make yourself. Charts may be helpful, but care must be taken so they do not appear too cold and businesslike. On the other hand, if you have one or more artists in the family you may be able to include both drawings and paintings from the past and ones made especially for this production. The artist(s) might be aware, though, that some styles of art are much

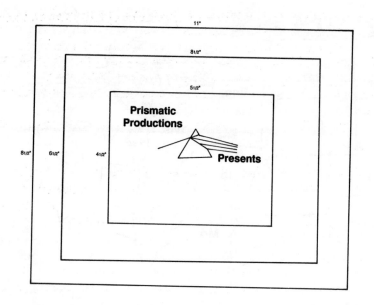

Illustration 9: How to display a graphic for best videotaped results

more effective for video than others. Cartoons and caricatures usually work well, while more intricate art may suffer as the detail is lost on the TV screen. Check how a certain type of art looks on the screen before spending a lot of time producing work which does not transfer well to video.

Whatever kind of graphics you want to make for your family video, there are certain guidelines to observe for best results. One of the most important of these is to use only the center of a sheet of paper or cardboard for your graphics of trees, drawings, maps, or whatever else is employed (see illustration 9). This illustration is similar to TV format; the proportions of the screen are a ratio of three vertical to four horizontal. You should produce graphics with the same format and proportions.

There are books written entirely about graphics for TV, so if you want to excel in this area it would be wise to read as much about the subject as possible before beginning. However, the information contained here is completely sufficient to show you how to produce graphics for your video. Experiment with different techniques, and do not become discouraged. You will be surprised, once you really use your imagination, how much creative graphics can add to a video production.

In-Camera Editing Techniques 4.3

A fundamental problem with producing quality video programs, using either the VHS or Beta formats, is that the videotape loses a certain amount of sharpness and clarity with each successive generation in the editing and copying process. You may have noticed this loss of resolution if you have ever seen home copies of movies or other material. Since some loss is inevitable from one generation to the next, every effort must be made to minimize the number of generations needed to produce a master tape. A clear master is essential because it will be used to make still another generation: the copies of the production which will be distributed to family members.

This "generational" problem is somewhat solved by using the technique of in-camera editing to produce the master. In-camera editing is not new; it is what most people with home cameras use. In fact, if you did not use two VCRs or some other editing setup to edit what you have shot with your camera, your video has been edited in-camera. The only difference is that when using the in-camera method to shoot the still visuals of the video master, the cuts and takes can be considered more seriously. If you are not completely satisfied with a take, simply rewind the tape and shoot the visual again until the take is just right. This type of in-camera editing, however, is usually not practical at the live shoot because the subjects can soon get bored and wooden if asked to repeat a take more than once. All of the still visuals, from photos to graphics, are shot on the master tape. Live segments, if any, are then added to the master using another VCR. By using this method copies of the finished production are only the first generation for the still material (especially important for those old photographs), and second generation for the live segments. This system results in the fewest possible generations to produce the completed program.

Before shooting the still visuals, a graphics board is needed for the operation. The graphics board is used to hold all of the still visuals in an upright position so they can be recorded by the video camera. Inexpensive graphic boards, which are also called easels, can be bought at art supply stores or made by a member of your crew (see illustration 10). We prefer the illustrated type of graphics board because it has a bottom groove and an adjustable top clip, which together serves to hold photos flat against the board. This becomes especially important for those small, old photographs that tend to curl from top to bottom. Also, the specially designed clip does not mar or poke holes in the visual material.

Whatever type of board you choose it should hold the visual upright, straight, and flat. The better the board can serve these functions the easier it will be to record your still visuals. If you are using hundreds of visuals, as we have sometimes done, imagine how important an efficient graphics board becomes. Often it is useful or necessary to place a weight on the base of the board to insure that the board will not shift position once it has been aligned perpendicular to the camera. Although lighting, as with any video recording, is of utmost importance for getting good results, one source of lighting is usually enough when shooting still visuals. A photo flood in a painter's scoop fixture, as described in section 3.1 (see page 17), will work. Use the clip on the scoop to fasten the light near the side of the camera so that the light points directly at the graphics board (see illustration 14, page 66). This eliminates any shadows around the visual.

Mount the camera on a tripod which is weighted so that it will not shake while operating the camera. Since many of the still visuals will be shot with the lens of the camera zoomed all the way in, the smallest movement of camera or visual becomes immediately noticeable in the playback.

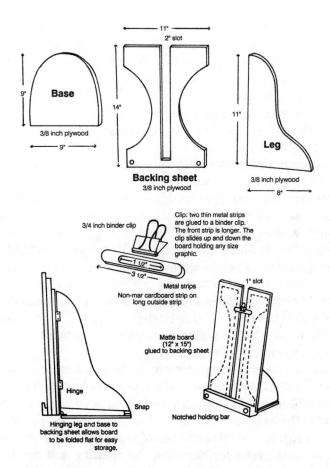

Illustration 10: A graphics board you can make yourself

Use a large TV or video monitor connected with the output of your camcorder or VCR to check how the visuals look on the screen before you record them. Make sure the camera is zoomed in enough so that no edges of the graphic shows on the screen. This can be deceptive since different TVs will frame the visuals differently and perhaps allow some edge to show. Also, inspect the visual for straightness on the screen. Here is where a graphics board with an adjustable clip, as illustrated, can be useful. A slight squeeze of the clip and the visual is instantly straightened. Some photos, especially the older ones, may be so small that the edges and clip show on the screen even after zooming in all the way with your camera. Before resigning yourself to recording them this way, move the camera, tripod and all, in closer to the graphics board to make sure you are as close to the visuals as possible while still remaining in focus.

As previously mentioned, the ratio format for TV is three vertical to four horizontal, so pictures and other visuals work best when they are also in this format, such as horizontal photos. Be sure to keep the essential information of your graphics in the center of the sheet.

As with any video recording, let the camera warm up for about ten minutes before white balancing the pickup tube. To white balance, clip a white card or piece of paper onto your graphics board which is illuminated with a photo flood bulb, and activate the white balance on the camera for a few seconds. Do this manually if possible, then check your "whiteness" on the TV screen.

Video cameras range greatly in the number of visual effects they offer the operator. Most cameras have a visual and audio fade capability which enables them to "fade up from black" at the beginning of a shot. The same feature also allows the operator to "fade down to black" at the end of the shot. The fade is most useful for denoting the opening and closing of several shots that make up a complete series within the production. The fade, however, can be used *too* often, lose its meaning, and become a distraction. If your camera doesn't have a fade feature you can still perform a fade manually if the camera has an adjustable iris. By closing the iris the camera fades to black. If you begin the recording with the iris closed and quickly and smoothly open it to the normal position, you can affect a fade up. Be careful not to shake the camera when executing a manual fade using the iris or when performing any other camera functions.

Carefully review the manual which came with your camera to see if it offers any options that you may never have used. Too often camera owners have not taken the time to learn all of the features of their cameras. For example, many cameras today feature systems for generating "internal titles." These can be extremely useful for labeling the still visuals you shoot. Practice dialing in the internal titles until you can do it swiftly and confidently. It will make changing the titles much easier when you begin recording numerous graphics and other still visuals per session. Some cameras also have a selection of colors to choose from when creating internal titles. Although white letters usually are easiest to see, try other colors that contrast with the background visual. To record internal titles on a black background, simply put on the lens cap. For other background variations, try sheets of paper of different colors on the graphics board.

Check your camera for a negative/positive feature; this permits the operator to use the camera to change what it records from positive to negative, and vice versa. While this might not initially seem useful, it can be very helpful for making small print, such as that normally found on invitations, much easier to read. This is because instead of black letters on a white background, the negative/positive switches it to white letters on a black background, which the eye can focus on much easier. The negative/positive feature also can work well with maps and other printed material, but it does not create a good effect on photos.

If your camera does not have internal title capabilities, you can still title at least some of the photographs by using external titles. Stationery stores sell sheets of transparent plastic, known as transparencies, which are used to project a drawn image on a screen with an overhead projector. The same stores also have rub-on or transfer letters of different sizes and styles. Choose a bold, block style that is at least one quarter inch high. Since most black and white photos are fairly dark, white letters often can be seen the best. Cut the transparencies the same size as the photo you wish to title and determine the best place or places to apply them. This method works very well for medium and large-sized photos, although it is rather time-consuming. When the transparency is clipped to the front of the photograph on the graphics board it becomes invisible, leaving only the lettering. Explore different styles and combinations but make sure that the labels are large enough to be read without strain on even a thirteen inch TV screen. (In fact, this should be the test for all of the graphics you intend to use in your family video.)

You can also create external titles and other written messages which have solid backgrounds. For this, use colored paper of a pastel shade and any type of bold lettering. Some people like stencils while others prefer rub-on letters or still some other method. Whichever you use, choose a bold style with both upper and lower case letters.

Another lettering option that is visually appealing is calligraphy. Having someone in the crew with a nice writing style fashion the external titles by using a felt tip pen or calligraphy brush and ink can make an excellent impression. This method is limited only by the creativity of the calligrapher, but remember to keep the lettering in the middle of the paper, following TV's three to four ratio format.

One problem with using a large number of still visuals in a video production is the lack of action it produces on the TV screen. After all, one cannot expect any movement from the subjects portrayed in a photograph. However, the camera operator can compensate for this shortage of action by injecting some camera movement into the process of recording still visuals. There are three basic camera movements which can be used to bring some action to still visuals:

1. Tilting (both up and down)
2. Panning (both right and left)
3. Zooming (both in and out)

You can also combine two or more of these camera movements with some of your visual material. You will find, as you experiment, that the smaller the subject the more restrictions there are on the camera movement. Again, the quality of the tripod head will have an effect on the ease of producing camera movement that does not suffer from shakes or jumps; a fluid head is greatly preferred.

We cannot overemphasize how much some creative camera movement can add to the professional look of your family video. The movement brings still material to life, especially if it is reserved for use once or twice in every four or five photos or graphics in a long series. The camera movement acquires meaning as it accentuates what the narrator is saying. For example, while the narrator talks about Grandmother at twenty, the photograph shown is a close-up of her face when she was about that age. As the narration continues with her marriage in 1924, the camera slowly zooms back to reveal a picture of Grandfather standing by her side, and it is their wedding day.

Each camera movement can be a distinct storytelling tool. A slow pan across an old photo shows the childrens' faces one by one as their names and birth dates are given by the narrator. If Aunt Gloria begins explaining one photo by drawing our attention to the boots she received as a gift when she was a girl, the camera should focus its attention there with a close-up of the boots for a moment, before tilting up to show the complete photo.

The story that goes with each photo or other still visual usually dictates the appropriate camera movement. Never miss an opportunity to use camera movement to lend emphasis to the story; it can sometimes be much more effective than words. A quick zoom in can be very dramatic by calling attention to some meaningful detail that the viewer might have missed.

Practice each camera move several times before rolling the tape, and if you are not completely satisfied with the result when you finally record, back up the tape and do it again. Usually you will know if you jerk, shake, or make other mistakes without looking at it. Make mental notes on some feature in the photograph that tells you when to stop zooming (especially out), so the border of the picture is not seen on the monitor.

Use your full creative powers to come up with camera movements that accent your production. The next time you watch the network news on TV notice how often they use photos and other still graphics to illustrate their stories. Take note of the camera movements they use and the effects they produce.

Make a list of all the different techniques you want to use with your in-camera editing. As your storyboard develops add notations indicating how you want to title and otherwise enhance certain visual material with camera movements. You can be confident that an increase in the number of special touches in your family video will result in a more interesting production.

4.4 Transferring Slides and Home Movies

Two other types of visual media that you can transfer to video in your home studio are slides and home movies. Both call for somewhat different techniques than those used with photographs and other still graphics.

Transferring slides to video is really not very difficult. Rather than using a graphics board as you did with the still visuals, the video camera instead records the slide from either the same screen normally used with a slide projector or, even better, a large white art card. The card and projector are the two additional pieces of equipment needed for transferring slides to video.

Since the highest quality slides transfer best to video, check them for even illumination, proper exposure, and be sure they are horizontally shot. As usual with video, subject matter with areas of high contrast between light and shadow will not shoot well. Remember to use the in-camera tips given in section 4.3 when you transfer slides. Camera movement is as important with slides as it is with other still visuals, and it is the surest way to make the slides as interesting as possible.

Keep the slide image on the screen smaller than you normally would when viewing them, because this will cause more light to be reflected back to the video camera. You will not be using any additional lighting when transferring slides to video, so it is important that the camera receive as much light as possible from the slide screen itself. Keep the projector and video camera as close to the screen as possible. Also, use a large video monitor or TV hooked up to your VCR or camcorder to keep an eye on the appearance of each slide before it is transferred (see illustration 11).

Transferring home movies to video is similar to transferring slides; they are shot while being projected onto a screen. As with slides, keep the image smaller than you usually would for viewing to keep the screen as bright as possible. The vast majority of home movies do not have an audio track, so leave the mike on your video camera unplugged and add your own sound later.

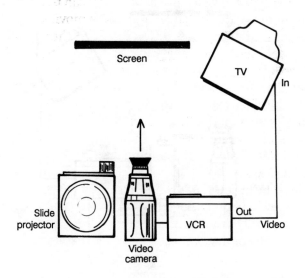

Illustration 11: Transferring 35mm slides to video

If you do happen to have Super 8mm or 16mm film with a sound track, transfer the sound at the same time you are transferring the picture. If your film projector has a line-out, use a patch cord from the line-out jack to your master VCR's MIC jack. If it does not have a line-out jack, use the external speaker jack with which most projectors are equipped. In this case you will probably have to keep the projector volume low (to avoid overload and distortion of the audio track), but it should work fine. Whether you use the line-out or speaker jack, be sure to use an attenuator in the line to protect your VCR. The attenuator, or pad as it is called, matches the speaker impedance to the line level of the VCR. The producer should use an attenuator whenever he or she connects sources of audio, such as other VCRs, audio amplifiers, tape players, etc., to the microphone jack of the master VCR (see illustrations 12 and 13). If your VCR did not come with an attenuator you can buy one at most electronic stores or dealers of your brand of VCR. Tell them what you intend to do with it and they will be able to help you.

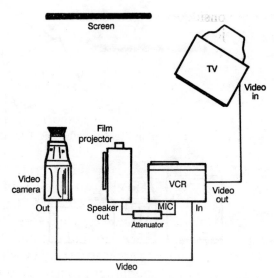

Illustration 12: Transferring home movies with or without sound to video

Illustration 13: Attenuator

One other consideration when transferring film to video is that film is projected at twenty-four frames per second, while video has thirty frames per second. Consequently, when film is transferred to video using an ordinary projector, there is a "flicker" effect on the video recording. The flicker can vary from unnoticeable, to slight, to distracting. If you are going to use only a short sequence or two of home movies in your production, you may choose just to tolerate the flicker.

If not, there are two solutions to this problem. The first, and more professional solution, is to find a projector fitted with either a five-blade shutter or a variable-speed shutter. These special shutters synchronize the speed of film with the video, eliminating the flicker. However, projectors fitted with these special shutters are difficult to find outside of professional media studios, and they are usually very expensive.

The second solution to the flicker problem is to increase slightly the projector's speed by routing the power cord through a variable voltage regulator. By increasing the voltage to the projector you can increase its running speed.

Many film projectors are equipped with speed control and also offer freeze frame, slow motion, and fast motion. These special effects may be used to make the production more interesting. Experiment with the projector's speed control to determine which setting allows the clearest and most flickerless video recording. Then, mark the projector with tiny pieces of tape so that you may return to "transfer speed" at any time.

Depending on the quality of the home movies you wish to include, the use of camera movement with the transfer can be especially important. Zooming in close on just part of the film picture can eliminate technical flaws, such as streaks of light that often mar home movies.

After working with video, film can seem particularly brittle and fragile, especially if the home movies are decades old. If the film is extremely valuable, make a practice video recording of it the first time you run it through the projector. You can then use the video copy to watch over and over while deciding where you want to make cuts, plan camera movement, etc. Use the sophistication of video technology as a tool to save wear and tear on old home movies and also as an editing aid to determine how best to treat them. Recording a practice tape will also allow you to refine your setup for transferring film to video.

When you are ready to add segments of the home movies to your master videotape, set your machine up in the following manner. The film should be cued up about five seconds before you want to record. The master videotape should also be cued, and the camera white balanced and ready. Unplug the camera mike and check your audio cable if you are transferring the audio track as well. Remember to account for the hesitation the VCR experiences once activated by the camera because of tape back-roll. Perfect your technique with the practice transfer and by using the least valuable and strongest roll of film. With some practice you will be able to make cuts that are well timed and smooth.

Some Options with Editing Equipment **4.5**

As we examine the equipment and hookups required for each editing option, refer to the illustrations of each option as you read the text. Every option will have both visual and audio hookups to consider.

Option Number One

You may use this option only if you do not have a live shoot (see illustration 14). In this case the video hookup is merely connecting the camera to the VCR or, if you are working with a camcorder, there are no hookups whatsoever. Simply get the unit ready and set up the graphics board, light, and monitor. If possible, leave the audio track blank while recording the visuals by unplugging the camera mike.

When editing the audio, your setup will depend on whether or not you use an audio mixer between your audio sources and the master VCR (the one with the AUDIO DUB feature). Illustration 15 shows the audio hookup without an audio mixer. The audio sources, i.e., audiocassette tape players, audio amplifiers, etc., are connected, via an attenuator, to the microphone jack of the master VCR. Audio levels must be controlled at their sources and "mixed" with a Y cord. This method takes some practice and patience but can yield satisfactory results in most cases.

However, as emphasized earlier, the audio mixer is the best way to overcome the restrictions of the VHS single audio track design. It allows you to both monitor and control your production closely. It is quite easy to add an audio mixer to the equipment you already are using. The mixer has a row of jacks labeled for different sources. Study the mixer manual before you make your purchase to be sure that the mixer has jacks of the correct kind and sufficient quantity needed. Again, ask the store personnel to help you if you have questions. Tell them the type of equipment you want to use with the mixer.

The audio mixer also has one or more output jacks. Use a patch cord with an attenuator to connect the main output jack of the mixer to the microphone jack of the master VCR. This centralizes the audio control and allows you to blend the audio sources up and down with a smoothness which is indistinguishable from professional productions.

The following three editing options add segments from the live video shoot to the in-camera master.

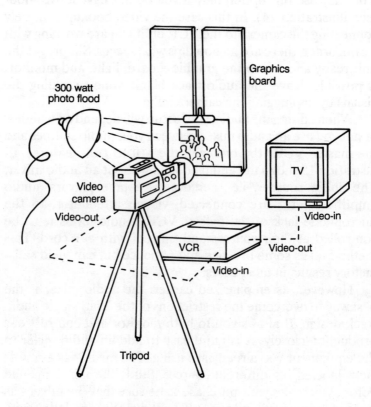

Illustration 14: Editing option one, i.e., in-camera editing; transferring still visuals to video

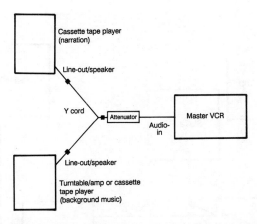

Illustration 15: Editing option one, audio hookup

Option Number Two

This incorporates two VCRs, a slave and a master, that each connect to their own monitors or TVs (see illustration 16). The connections go from the slave VCR out to a Y cord which sends the signal to both a monitor/TV and the video-in of the master VCR. The slave VCR audio-out is run through an attenuator to the microphone jack of the master VCR. If you are using an audio mixer, treat the audio output of the slave VCR as you would any audio source. An audio mixer can also be used with options three and four which follow.

Option Number Three

This option introduces the piece of video equipment you might consider acquiring if you already have an audio mixer. It is a video switcher and special effects generator (SEG). If you think this will explode your production budget, let us assure you that the Hybrid-8, a simple switcher, enhancer, and SEG, is priced low enough for the home enthusiast. In fact, there are several makes and models of switchers and SEGs, some combined in one unit and some not, that are comparable to the Hybrid-8, and priced at a few hundred dollars. If you would

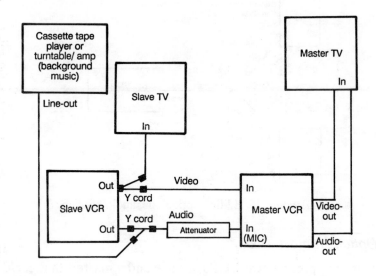

Illustration 16: Editing option two; basic editing format using only two VCRs and an additional audio source for background music

like more information about the Hybrid-8 write to: Video Interface Products, 19310 Ecorse Road, Allen Park, MI 48101.

A video switcher is similar to an audio mixer except that the video switcher primarily works with visual signals. The optimum setup when using a video switcher is to have two slave VCRs feeding into the switcher and out to the video-in of the master VCR, but it also is useful with only two VCRs, one master and one slave (see illustration 17).

The SEG allows you to choose from a variety of visual "wipes" of transition, which connect one sequence to the next. So instead of the straight cut from one visual to the next, the producer can fade down with certain visual wipes and fade up to the next visual with the same or a different visual wipe. Used sparingly in the appropriate places, these special effects can

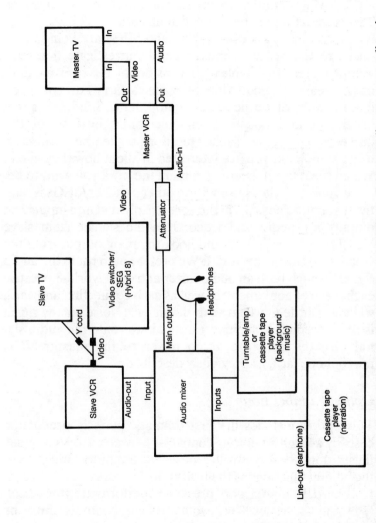

Illustration 17: Editing option three; audio/video editing with two VCR's and three audio sources, audio mixer and video switcher/SEG

smooth the transition from one setting or subject to the next. Used excessively, they can become disconcerting and distracting, drawing attention to the medium and not the message. This is something to be avoided at all costs.

Since new types of switchers and SEGs are being introduced to the market almost monthly, investigate the latest written material available when considering this type of equipment. Nearly all good video magazines carry advertising on many kinds of audio/video equipment. Send for some brochures and talk with an electronics buff about the numerous choices available. Question people who are already using equipment you are interested in about how they like it. Watch them use it, keeping in mind the work you want to do.

Connecting the Hybrid-8 and other switcher/SEGs is relatively simple. The jacks in the back are divided into inputs and outputs for audio and video. Join the signals from slave VCR(s) to video inputs, and hook the main output from the switcher to the master VCR. We prefer not to route the audio signal through both an audio mixer and our Hybrid-8 because each piece of equipment, as well as each connection and cord, will add a little more noise to the signal. (Noise on any signal is to be absolutely avoided.) Instead, we route the audio signal directly from the audio mixer to the master VCR microphone jack, as previously described.

Option Number Four

This option includes the first dramatic jump in production costs by adding an editing controller between two VCRs (see illustration 18). A controller allows the editor to control all of the editing functions of the two VCRs from a centralized control board. Edit points are preset and performed automatically by the controller. The two VCRs and controller must be compatible, and, in fact, it is best to buy all three as a unit. Although the cost of a controller has dropped in the last couple of years, it will still add a minimum of three thousand dollars to your equipment costs. While this is considered inexpensive

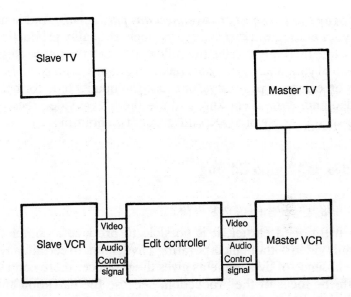

Illustration 18: Editing option four; format using an edit controller

by professional video production standards, it is generally beyond the budget of all but the most determined video devotee. As with switchers and SEGs, controllers differ with make and model, so investigate them as you would any other serious investment.

New video equipment designed and priced for the home consumer is appearing on the market daily. For example, there are new titlers which are incredibly versatile tools for adding animation and graphics of all kinds and are now priced as low as one thousand dollars, something unheard of just months ago. The easiest way to avoid large investment costs, however, is to find audio/video facilities that offer rental time on this kind of sophisticated equipment. Usually the actual editing is either performed or assisted by a professional video technician, depending on the experience of the customer.

In all of your audio/video hookups consult the operator's manuals that are supplied with such equipment and use the highest quality patch cords. *Make sure all equipment is turned off before you connect or disconnect any patch cords.* And in all of your editing work, strive for the highest quality production possible by remembering the following: keep the heads clean on all of your audio and visual recording equipment; clean lenses on cameras, projectors, etc.; use top quality tape for both video and audio recording; and use the fastest video recording speed, i.e., SP or STANDARD PLAY (two hour mode).

4.6 Video and Audio Editing

Editing without Live Segments

As mentioned earlier, it is possible to produce a complete family video without incorporating a live shoot. In certain ways the absence of live segments gives the producer more control with the focus of the production, because the narration and other audio recordings are the only vehicles for telling the family's story. The selection and order of the visual material also play a larger part in shaping the theme when live segments are not used.

Before you begin recording the visuals you should have a clear and comprehensive storyboard. Every visual must have a "block" on the storyboard that contains the duration each will be recorded, any camera movement, and the transitions leading into and out of the visuals (see illustration 2, page 38). The storyboard ought also to include any intended use of titles, both external and internal, and their duration on the screen. Finally, have a complete record of the audio cues which will be used to time the visuals. In fact, a good copy of the narration on audiocassette is needed. And you are now ready to begin editing your video.

With your video camera's lens and VCR heads cleaned, set up your equipment as shown in illustration 14 (see page 66). As your camera warms up, fine-tune the exact positioning of each piece of equipment, weighting them down once their proper spot is found.

Break the seal on the videotape that will become your production master. Place the tape in the VCR or camcorder and switch it to FAST FORWARD, rewinding it either automatically or manually when it reaches the end. This is good to do with any new tape because it adjusts the tape's tension to the machine.

Next, lay a black track on the tape by recording with the video camera while leaving its lens cap on. The black track makes it easier for future images to "grab on" to the videotape at edit points. We recommend that you lay a black track on the complete length of your master tape. This will take two hours (T120 tape on SP mode), and you can either record the black track at an earlier time or spend the two hours putting the final polish on the production plans.

After recording the two hours of black, make sure the tape is completely rewound; sometimes the tape will not be entirely at the end, so check it. Then, with the machine on PLAY, check the black track for uniformity and to see if it meets with your satisfaction. Real video zealots recommend that the entire two hours of the black track be visually examined for defects or dropouts in the tape itself. We have never been able to submit to such tedious scrutiny, preferring instead to use the highest professional quality tape available.

Rewind the tape again to the very beginning. Put the VCR on PLAY again, but for only fifteen seconds, then push STOP. Set your first visual on the graphics board, and arrange the visuals which follow in correct order, laying them out in close proximity to the board. Try to record twenty to thirty visuals every time the camera is "up," meaning, while the VCR is on PAUSE and the camera is ready to shoot. Then, rewind the tape and review what has been shot. If, however, something goes wrong with a particular visual and the result is suspect, review it right then. There is no reason to continue if you will eventually have to go back and reshoot because you are dissatisfied with an earlier edit. Be careful at all times, because the recording tab is in the videotape, making it possible to erase all or parts of it at any time. Remember when reviewing your edits that it is easy to wipe a section out accidently. Because you will be adding the audio track in a distinct and separate step of production, it is best to leave the mike on the camera unplugged. While it is not important if it cannot be unplugged, you will have to be extremely careful to erase the audio track completely before adding the production sound track you have made.

Regarding your first visual, many home producers find difficulty in getting started. One clever way is to make up a logo and name for your "production company," and begin with a graphic such as illustration 9 (see page 52). There may be a family nickname to incorporate in the production name, or there may be a particular location of importance in the family history. The logo graphic introduces the title shot. Internal titles over a symbolic photo work well as the title shot, or you can also use a transparency to create an external title over an appropriate photo as described earlier.

It is extremely important to use a stopwatch to time precisely the length each visual is recorded, taking into account the camcorder or VCR's back-roll time. Develop and practice a routine which allows you to record several visuals in sequence with minimal stress. The timing of the audio track dictates the timing of the visual track. A second or two off may seem trivial, but by the tenth or eleventh visual the timing will be off by enough seconds to throw the visual track out of synchronization with the audio track. To keep the two synchronized it is best to add the proper audio track after recording about ten minutes of visuals. This serves to keep the audio and visual mediums balanced. The next part of this section, "Recording an Audio Track on Video with Prerecorded Visuals," explains how to perform these techniques in detail.

The final word when editing, whether by the in-camera method or any other, is to check every edit. Only when you are satisfied should you continue. You may find that some edits will have a "rainbow effect," vertical streaks of color, for the first few seconds. This is caused by the VCR getting "up to speed," and is considered normal. In fact, the only way to avoid rainbows is to use an editing system which utilizes a controller, and even then the elimination is not 100 percent effective. When you are working with half inch videotape, either VHS or Beta, network quality productions are simply not possible, especially after a few generations.

To compensate partially for this, review section 4.3, "In-Camera Editing Techniques," before you begin your master. The more techniques you use in your family video the more interesting it will be. Utilize the full artistic potential of the video medium to create a production which will repeatedly captivate audiences.

Recording an Audio Track on Video with Prerecorded Visuals

It is a challenge to record a creative sound track with the VHS format because of its single audio track. Because of this, all audio to be recorded on the master must be blended before it reaches the master VCR. This is not a problem with the Beta format, which has two audio tracks, or with all wider, professional video formats, which have two or more audio tracks.

Review section 4.1, "A Creative Audio Track," to refresh your memory about the different options available in the recording process. In that chapter three methods are given for "mixing" the narration and background music into a single signal before recording it as the master audio track from the master VCR. The first is to play the background music while the narration is being recorded on audiocassette. This method has the least control and most questionable quality. The second uses a Y cord to mix the two signals, and the third and superior method makes use of an audio mixer. All three methods break the narration into approximately ten minute blocks, and each method requires fading the background music until it is completely off by the time the narrator has reached the end of each block. The narrator should begin each block alone, with the operator pausing momentarily before slowly fading up the background music. This allows the blocks to be joined on the video master with little notice, provided the volume levels of all audio sources remain constant.

As we examine three ways to hook up an audio track to the master videotape, refer to the corresponding illustrations. First is the hookup without an audio mixer (see illustration 19). If your background music is recorded on a cassette tape you will need two cassette tape players, one for the background music and one for the recorded narration. If the backgound music is on a record you will need a turntable and amplifier along with one tape player for the narration. Whether tape player or amp, check to see if they are equipped with line-out jacks or speaker jacks, either of which can be used.

If neither of these jacks are present your units should have a headphone jack, which can be used with a patch cord that connects to one of the double female jacks of a Y cord. Plug the Y cord into the proper attenuator, and plug the attenuator into the microphone jack of your master VCR. Connect the

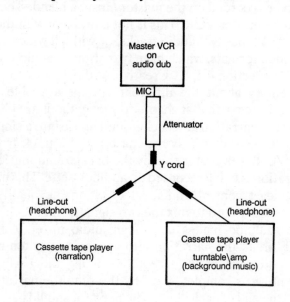

Illustration 19: Mixing two audio sources using a Y cord

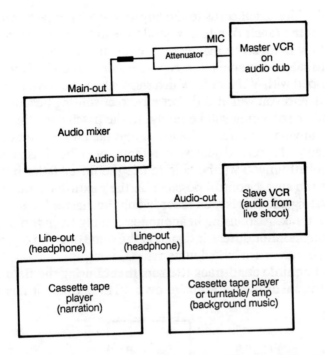

Illustration 20: Mixing three audio sources using an audio mixer

other jack of the Y cord to either the line-out jack or the headphone jack of the cassette tape player; it will play the narration. The main problem with using a Y cord is that the sound
is hard to monitor and mix well. Start with the volume on the
source machine, either tape player or amp, set low, and slowly increase it while using the headphones plugged into the
audio-out of the master VCR or by listening to the master
TV/monitor. Practice your technique until you are satisfied
with your results.

The second audio hookup uses the service of an audio
mixer (see illustration 20). As described earlier, the mixer
takes two or more audio input signals and combines them into
a single output. Using the same outputs from your audio
amplifier and tape player(s) that you would using a Y cord,

connect the patch cords to the appropriate input jacks on the back of the mixer. While it is good to read the mixer's manual carefully before you make your connections, the input jacks are usually very similar in capacity. Most audio mixers are equipped with VU meters which show when you have the best signal, and you will also detect incorrect routing because the sound or recording will be faulty. In the patch cord that connects the main output of the mixer and the audio input of the master VCR there should be an attenuator. When it is properly hooked up you will be able to use the mixer fader bars to exert the surest control possible on the mixture of the audio output signal. This is then recorded on the master VCR as the audio track. Also, using headphones coming from the mixer, you can monitor different signals at the same time, both before and after they are switched to the main output.

The third sound-track hookup, that of using the Beta format, has a distinct advantage over VHS because it has two

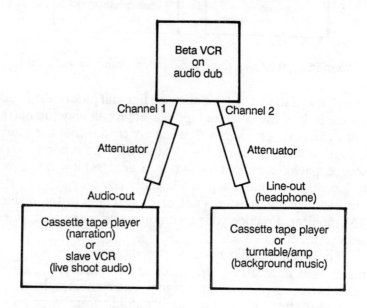

Illustration 21: Recording two audio sources on Beta

audio tracks (see illustration 21). This allows you to add the narration block by block, and then return uninterrupted to the beginning of the master to add the background music. Not only is the background music easier to add this way, but the end product has a much smoother quality. Although an audio mixer may be used with the Beta format, it is also possible to connect the sources of audio directly to the separate channels of the Beta master VCR. (Again use an attenuator for each line.) Make sure that the two audio channels are individully switched so you will be able to record different channels at different times. Again, read the VCR manual carefully to discover the full range of options available for audio editing. Polish your editing technique with some practice material before producing your family video.

The AUDIO DUB feature on the master VCR allows the editor to record an audio track onto the videotape without in any way disturbing the visuals previously recorded. A word of caution: it is easy to activate the PLAY/RECORD mode of the master VCR when using the AUDIO DUB. If this happens the recorded visuals will be erased, and you will have to begin again from the point of erasure. Remember to make a firm distinction between the two procedures and do not confuse them during editing.

Before you begin recording your production master audio track make sure the audio track on the master tape is "clean." To do this, rewind the tape *completely* and activate the AUDIO DUB/PLAY mode of the master VCR with *no* audio or video inputs to the master VCR. Then, when you have cleaned the audio track just past the visuals, rewind the tape again and listen to it for any "bumps" or other unwanted sounds on the audio track. When you are satisfied rewind the master tape one more time to begin recording the master audio track.

As shown in illustrations 19, 20, and 21, you will usually have two audio sources, one for the narration and one for the background music, feeding audio signals into your master VCR. Both sources must first be cued to their correct position by winding them to about one or two seconds before they are to be recorded on the master tape. It is a little harder to cue a phonograph record than it is a cassette tape, but with a little practice you will succeed. The exact timing of the background music is not quite as crucial as the narration.

When you have the two source machines cued, set the master VCR AUDIO DUB/PLAY mode at the *beginning* of the tape. Remember, you have ten to fifteen seconds of black track before the video fades up to the first visual. Start bringing the background music up to its predetermined volume a couple of seconds before your first visual appears, and then begin the narration at the appropriate time. Monitor the volumes of the audio sources as closely as possible, using the external speaker of the master TV/monitor if you are not using an audio mixer with headphones.

Another nice feature of many mixers is that it allows the operator to monitor the volumes of various signals *before* the signals are mixed and sent to the master VCR. With a mixer, begin the recording process with the main output mixer completely down to avoid producing a whine on the master tape.

Once the two source machines are rolling fade up the main output of the mixer while leaving the source channels at predetermined levels. Practice will enable you to create a smooth and professional sounding audio track. As previously mentioned, fade out the background music before you reach the end of the audio block you are recording.

These blocks should be about ten minutes in duration. If they run any longer the audio track becomes difficult to keep synchronized with the visuals. If you are going to record ten minute blocks of audio you must record visuals that are somewhat longer in duration, because the audio track is always added to prerecorded visuals, never the other way around. In other words, the audio track can never extend beyond where the visuals have ended. This is because it is impossible to record visuals of any kind on VHS videotape without erasing any previously recorded audio. Seconds before the block of narration ends, fade down the background music. When the narration reaches the end of the block quickly fade off that channel of the mixer also, but there is no rush to pause the master VCR. In fact, letting it run a couple of seconds without any audio input signal guarantees a clean audio track between the audio blocks. A clean audio track will join the pieces of narration so smoothly that no one will realize it was recorded on the master tape in blocks.

When adding audio segments recorded on cassette tapes by relatives to the video master, treat them just like the narration. Add the same background music as that used behind the narration and make an effort to match the volume levels of these different tapes when you transfer them to the video master.

After recording the audio block behind some visuals, return to more in-camera editing. Again, disconnect all audio sources from the camcorder or camera VCR and proceed to record more visuals. When you have recorded the visuals further than your next audio block, go back to recording the audio on the master tape. The editing is a continuum, first recording a block of visuals with the camera, then adding the audio track, and repeating this process until the video is complete.

As with the building of anything else, the quality of all the different pieces either enhance or detract from the completed effort. Keep your standards high and do not hesitate to re-edit, either the visual or audio, if you are not fully satisfied. Use both the audio and visual mediums to their fullest potential to create an interesting and informative program. Check all of your edits frequently, because once you move on with your editing it is impossible to correct an earlier mistake without also redoing *everything* recorded after the mistake.

If you do not plan to add any live video, this is the complete process. Just continue adding blocks of visuals and then blocks of audio until you approach the end of the story you are showing and telling. Before you reach your final visual, read chapter 5, "Wrapping the Production: Finishing Touches."

Combination Editing: Still Visuals and Background Music with the Audio/Visuals from a Live Shoot

The editing process is quite different if you add audio/visual material from a live shoot to the still visuals produced by the in-camera editing techniques just discussed. While the equipment options are listed in section 4.5, "Some Options with Editing Equipment," the combination editing basically calls for the use of another VCR and TV/monitor. Here we will examine some general editing techniques which can be used with an assortment of equipment setups, but each have a minimum of two VCRs and two or three audio sources.

The cardinal rule is to get to know your editing equipment. This can be a problem if you are renting some of the gear, so try to rent equipment with which you are most comfortable. This is particularly crucial when editing with two VCRs, because you must know their individual back-roll times. Back-roll is the length of time, usually a second or two, that it takes a VCR to actually begin recording after the operator releases the PAUSE button which begins the RECORD/PLAY mode. It also occurs when a VCR is activated by a camera. When editing, a second or two can make a tremendous difference in how the cut looks and sounds.

One measuring device to aid you with timing your editing points is the VCR's tape counter. The counter is most effective when used in conjunction with the counter/memory feature. When rewinding, the VCR will automatically stop at 0000 when the memory function has been activated. This means that the editor can automatically rewind both master and slave VCRs back to the beginning of every edit. When making an edit watch the counter of the master VCR for the number of counts it rewinds (usually just one or two) before it moves forward and records.

You should be aware of two effects that the VCR back-roll creates. First, it erases the last second or two of the end of the previous recording, both audio and visual tracks. The second effect of the back-roll is the formation of "rainbows" along the vertical edge of the video image. Rainbows usually last only a second or two and are not often distracting, which is good since they are virtually impossible to avoid with most half inch (VHS and Beta) video editing. Remember, network studios use hundreds of thousands of dollars worth of equipment and scores of technicians to produce the familiar TV programs we watch. While following the methods described in this book will not achieve network results, they will help produce a video that you and your family can enjoy with pride.

Adding segments from the live shoot to a master with visuals already on it is not difficult. Arrange the slave VCR and TV/monitor, the master VCR and its TV/monitor, and any other equipment you are using in such a way so that editing is as comfortable and easy as possible (see illustration 22). If one of the VCRs you are using for editing is also the one you are using with the camera, disconnect the camera before you begin editing. After checking all your connections use a tape other than the master to make a practice edit which includes all of the techniques, both audio and visual, that you intend to perform on the family video master.

If you want to add background music behind the voices on the live shoot segments, it must be done at the same time you are recording the visual and/or audio live shoot segments to the master tape. Make sure the background music is the same volume level at peak loudness as it is with the narration. Plus, the live voices should be the approximate volume level of the narration. *The matching of audio levels and smoothness of cuts are the primary determinants for producing a quality audio track.*

Once you are satisfied with your practice edits place the master tape, which may already have some still visuals and narration recorded on it, in the master VCR. The videotape from the live shoot should be in the slave VCR and cued at the proper place, which is about five seconds before the beginning of the segment you want to add to the master tape. If the audio from the live shoot is to be included make sure the audio line from the slave VCR is routed properly to the master VCR. Determine all volume levels in advance and have the back-

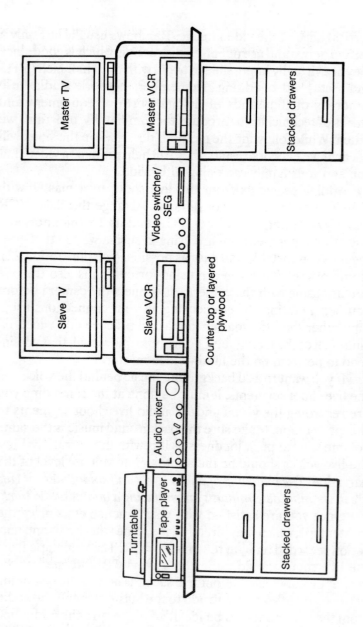

Illustration 22: A view of an editing station

ground music cued and properly routed. Set the slave VCR tape counter to 0000 and activate the counter memory. Cue the master tape in the master VCR by first placing it on PLAY to review the last thirty seconds of the previously recorded segment. When the tape reaches the edit point where the live segment is to be added, *accounting for back-roll time,* put the master VCR on PAUSE, and prepare the machine to record by pressing PLAY/RECORD. Now is when it is important to have correctly calculated the back-roll time of the master VCR. It enables you to know how much of the previous segment will be recorded over; it is a second or two *before* the point where the tape is set on PAUSE.

Try to plan edits in places on the tape where the timing does not have to be precise. We have achieved a clean cut when editing together live segments by using the master VCR AUDIO DUB feature. It can erase the audio track on the master tape an instant after the last desired word is spoken. It is the audio track which is the most likely to mar cuts by either clipping the end of the last sentence or by getting the first syllable of the next unwanted word. Erasing the audio track at the proper point gives you a small breathing space, allowing you to make the edit without the worry of leaving or erasing some of the audio track by mistake. Also, this is usually a much more precise operation than editing both audio and visual with two VCRs. Just make sure not to cut off any of the new audio by starting the edit a second late (by releasing PAUSE on the master VCR late). Since home VCRs do not usually have a volume control on the audio output, you cannot adjust the volume level of the slave VCR unless you are using an audio mixer or are routing the output through an audio amplifier. Adjust the volumes of all audio sources to match the volume level of the slave VCR, since it is the least controllable audio source.

After erasing the unwanted audio and setting the PAUSE about one second ahead of where you want to cut to the new segment, you are ready to set the master VCR at the proper edit point. Set the tape counter of the master VCR to 0000 and activate its memory. Switch the cued slave VCR to PLAY and closely watch the slave monitor. A second or two *before* you want to cut to the slave tape release the PAUSE button of the master VCR, which will back-roll and then begin recording. At the same moment the master monitor will show the beginning edit point. If you are using a mixer make sure all your fader bars are eased up to the proper volume levels at the end of the back-roll of the master VCR. If you want to add the background music to the live audio slowly fade the music up (to the levels predetermined when recording the narration onto the master videotape) soon after the voice of the speaker begins. Keep the background music soft so it does not interfere with the understanding of the narration. Fade the music completely out before the next edit point so it will not cut off abruptly. Let the new segment run slightly past the next edit point, because it will give you some space in which to work. *Remember, too long of a "tail" is preferrable to one too short.* The slave VCR is not on PAUSE at or before the edit point, but instead the audio visual signals it puts out are recorded by the master VCR "on the roll." By doing this the editor has only to compensate for the back-roll of the master VCR, not both the master and slave.

When the edit is complete bring the master and slave VCRs to STOP. With the tape counter and memory set on the master VCR you can simply press REWIND and it will automatically return to the beginning of the edit you just made. The tape should be rewound far enough to give you time to scrutinize thoroughly the edit point. Listen carefully for any bumps or other imperfections on the audio track. Make sure you can hear the speakers clearly, and check the background music for correct volume, ensuring that it is not cut off abruptly at the end. *Be completely satisfied with your results before you decide to move on.* One excellent feature of video is that nothing is lost in the editing process except time. Going back over an edit is as easy as rewinding both of the VCRs and repeating the process outlined above.

With re-editing comes one condition: begin the second take slightly before your first take. This does not usually present a problem if you erase the last second or two of the previous audio segment, thereby granting a little slack at your edit points. Allow as many takes as you need to obtain satisfactory results. This can be done until you actually start cutting off the end of the last finished segment. It does tend to reduce frustration, however, if you can get the look and sound you are working for in the fewest number of tries.

When you are satisfied with the editing refer to the storyboard for the next segment. If it is another segment from the live shoot video the editor consults the live shoot log, recorded on shoot day, to find the desired segment in the live shoot tapes. The editor, at this point, will truly appreciate the log's clearly numbered and indexed account of the live shoot tapes.

Remember as you shuttle the tapes back and forth, the recording tab is still in and the live shoot tapes can be accidentally erased. This is even more serious than erasing part of the master tape, because the master can be produced again, while the tapes from the live shoot are irreplaceable unless you schedule another shoot. Since you can lose the video material only through your own neglect and mistakes, be careful during the editing process.

If the next section to edit consists of still visuals rather than another live segment, it may or may not be necessary to unhook the VCR from your editing equipment while working with the camera. With the slave VCR's power off, try using the camera. If this does not work and you must disconnect the master VCR from the editing setup, it is not difficult to rehook it up for editing.

Before you begin to record stills again, you may want to review section 4.3, "In-Camera Editing Techniques." One clever technique is to cut from a family member speaking at the live shoot to a still of the same person years before, while his or her voice continues its narration. This can make a moving and startling visual transition and reveal the type of creativity afforded with the video medium. It is also an example of the dramatic spark which can make your family video production come to life!

Recording Live Shoot Audio with Background Music behind Still Visuals

This last general editing technique, recording segments of audio captured at the live shoot behind still visuals, can produce some of the most captivating footage in the production. As family members talk about different photos, these very snapshots appear on the TV screen, coming alive as never before. In section 4.3, "In-Camera Editing," recall how you timed the still visuals with the narration. For this editing technique you time the still visuals so that they will be synchronized with the speakers from the live shoot. It might be helpful to review section 4.3 to refresh your memory to the various details of the process. As explained there, each visual's time on the screen is recorded on the storyboard across from the audio cues at the beginning and end (see illustration 2, page 38). Remember to take the VCR's back-roll time into account when recording the visuals or you will lose a second or two of each visual, spoiling your synchronization. After recording the last visual let the tape run to about five seconds beyond the end of the audio and then stop it. Rewind the master tape back to the point where the audio from the live shoot is to begin.

Check the audio ending of the previous block segment. Use the AUDIO DUB feature (as described earlier) to clean the audio track by erasure. Now check for the proper audio hookups. Illustrations 19 (see page 76), 21 (see page 78), and 23 show the equipment chains with and without an audio mixer. Patch your equipment together so that the slave VCR's audio channel and the background music source, either an audio amp or tape player, are both connected to the microphone jack of your master VCR. Always use the proper audio attenuator for your master VCR to protect it from audio input signals too strong for the VCR to handle. When everything is hooked up correctly and you have made a couple of satisfactory test recordings, cue up the audio sources that will be combined to create your master audio track.

Without an audio mixer you must control the volume of the background music at the source, so begin with its volume turned all the way down. You cannot control the volume of the slave VCR audio track whatsoever, so make all other audio levels, including the narration, tapes from other family members, the background music, and any other segment with sound, close to the volume of the slave VCR.

Audio dubs can usually be made much more accurately than visual edits. Set the slave VCR to a few seconds before the beginning of the audio you want to record on the background music. It is best to use background music that can be faded up at any point and still sound fine. Use the speaker of the slave TV/monitor and the speaker of the tape player to "tell" you when to begin the audio dub on the master VCR. But first, the master VCR must be precisely paused at the end of

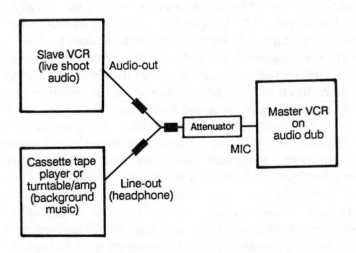

Illustration 23: Mixing live shoot audio with background music

the last recorded audio block and the AUDIO DUB feature activated.

The slave VCR is put on PLAY while the master VCR is on PAUSE. Be ready to release the PAUSE button a second or two *before* hearing what you want to record from the slave VCR audio track. When both VCRs are running evenly, the slave on PLAY and the master on AUDIO DUB, slowly and smoothly increase the volume on the background music. Marking the volume level on the equipment with tape or pencil, keep the music low enough so it does not interfere with understanding the speaker. Turn the background music completely down before you reach the end of the last sentence of the audio block from the live shoot. An audio mixer is valuable here because it centralizes all the volume controls, the volumes of the input tracks and the main line output. Dexterity of motion is required if you do not have a mixer, but with practice you will be able to perfect your movements and produce pleasing audio tracks.

We offer a few helpful tips for you to remember for all audio editing. If you do use a mixer employ the whole range of its features. For example, use it not only to fade down the background music before the end of the spoken part, but also to fade the speaker's voice when reaching the end of the point you wish to record. This will automatically create that clean audio tail which eases the addition of the next audio segment. In a nutshell, try to begin and end all audio recordings without an audio "load" going into the master VCR; i.e., when it is taken off PAUSE at the beginning of the edit and put onto AUDIO DUB at the end of the process the input level should be at zero. The "load" results from having the volume up on one of the audio sources, and, even though there is no actual sound, it usually produces a buzzing noise. Keep detailed audio notes with precise volume settings for each piece of equipment. This will help you create an interesting sound track for your family video which is also technically consistent.

Editing Summary

The editing process is the heart and soul of the video production. With any format you choose there are several techniques that you can use to make a family video for which you can be proud. Although the video medium offers the producer a wide range of creative options, the technical limitations of the VHS, and to a lesser extent Beta, must be recognized and resolved. Do not be crushed by your first editing attempts. As with any other skill, it takes some practice to produce pleasing results. Make every effort to plan your edits in places that allow as much time as possible and yet still look good. That is the reason for our recommendation of cleaning the audio track after each block. Try to do your editing when you have enough time so you are not rushed. Editing often requires far more time than one might think, so you may find yourself spending more hours editing than originally anticipated. Once you hone your skills, however, editing can be quite fun.

Be realistic about the results you want to achieve, especially if you tend to be a perfectionist. On the other hand, try not to sacrifice your standards unless you face a technical obstacle that only more sophisticated equipment can overcome. Your greatest allies are ingenuity and perseverance. With imagination and a little elbow grease you will be able to produce a family video that reaches far beyond most expectations.

When practicing the editing techniques you intend to use in the video, involve the members of the family who have expressed an interest in the editing process. While it is sometimes difficult to retain production continuity with more than one editor, the problem is lessened if the various editors have shared the responsibilities of producing a good storyboard. The important point to remember is that versatility and flexibility are usually of more value to the production effort than technical considerations.

CHAPTER FIVE

Wrapping the Production: Finishing Touches

The Ending Visuals 5.1

You may think that by now you have learned all the necessary steps to produce your family video. Almost, but not quite. What about adding the credits and letting your audience know who worked on the production?

Credits can be added to the production by using several methods. Perhaps the simplest is to arrange a stack of light cardboard sheets on your easel, each with a credit written in the center and then "pulling" them at timed intervals. The pulling takes a little patience and skill to avoid shaking the easel and the rest of the credits while removing the top one, but with practice you can make each pull look like a cut. Since your in-camera editing techniques, by this time, have been perfected, you can also use the video camera to make the cuts from credit to credit. Try to keep the duration on each credit fairly uniform and make sure each credit is centered and straight on the screen. Another method is to use a flip-chart and let the credits fall into place on an easel in front of the rolling camera.

While using the camera's internal titles may seem a good idea, there are usually enough credits to make it a lengthy and tedious process. If you do opt for this method make sure you use an interesting picture(s) as the background. Although we find internal titling too awkward for long credits, we do use it to create "The End" over the last still visual, typically a symbolic photograph of the family.

Producing credits can also be done in more elaborate ways. One nice technique is to make the credits either crawl (horizontal movement) or roll (vertical movement) across the screen. To make credits crawl use a large piece of posterboard with two vertical slots cut in it (see illustration 24). The credits are printed in bold letters on a roll of computer, or similar,

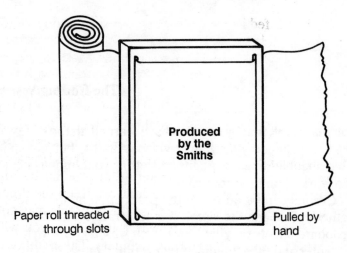

Paper roll threaded
through slots

**Produced
by the
Smiths**

Pulled by
hand

Illustration 24: Pull-board used to produce crawl or verticle roll

Titles go here

Illustration 25: Using a turntable for a mechanized credit crawl

paper, and then fed into the slots on either side of the poster-board. The slots keep the paper straight and tight across the board, and the board is anchored by books or bricks to keep it from moving during the recording. We have found with this method, however, that it is difficult to pull the credits through in one long, smooth pull. Instead, they have a tendency to snag and jump on occasion. To minimize this problem and produce an even crawl it is necessary to mechanize the process. One way to do this is to use an old turntable. You may need a spacer cylinder to raise the cardboard credit drum (see illustration 25) so that it is above the turntable controls. Keep the drum and spacer as light as possible because the turntable may not rotate if they are too heavy. However light it is, you will probably still have to start its turning manually. The credits are again printed in bold letters on computer paper, which is at-tached to the outside of the drum. With some experimentation this method can be quite satisfactory, although there is a limit to the number of credits which will fit on the drum.

One more rather unique method of producing a credit crawl is to use a chain of wheeled pull-toys. If the toys are large enough, cards can be taped to their sides. As the toys are pulled across a table, each credit passes in front of the camera (see illustration 26).

Vertical rolls are also a very pleasing technique for presenting credits. The easiest way to produce a credit roll is similar to the crawl, which uses a stiff piece of posterboard with a paper slot on two edges (see illustration 27). For the vertical, however, the slots are placed on the top and bottom edges of the firmly anchored posterboard. Unfortunately, this roll suffers from the same problem as the crawl design; it is extremely hard to pull the entire length of credits through the board without some hesitations, slowdowns, and jumps. Even after installing a hand-cranked roll we could not produce a credit roll that was as slow and smooth as desired.

As with the crawl, the answer to the problem is mechanization. Design a mount on one side of the roll-board, shaped from layers of plywood, to hold a variable-speed power drill (see illustration 27). Found in many garages and tool sheds, this common power tool can probably be borrowed for a couple of days if you do not own one. As its name implies, a

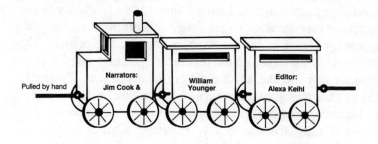

Illustration 26: Using a pull-toy to make credits crawl

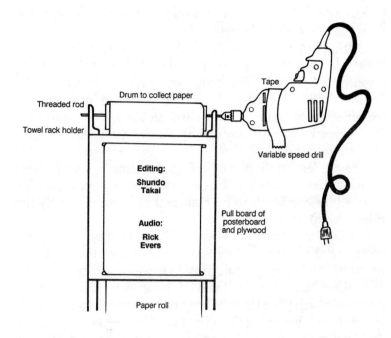

Illustration 27: Credit roll mechanized with power drill

variable-speed drill's speed can be adjusted with a screw lock on the trigger. This allows you to have the credits roll as slowly as you wish. The drum of the roll can be made by passing a threaded rod through an empty oatmeal box, and wrapped twice around with light poster board both to stiffen and lengthen it. Secure the oatmeal box to the threaded rod and support the rod with towel rack holder brackets as both ends. Chuck one end of the rod into the drill. Leaving a long blank lead-in before the credits start will allow you to adjust the speed of the drill before the credits are in front of the camera. Make sure the credit board is well lighted with a 300 watt photo flood or similar lighting. If you are able to use a typesetter, the credits can be typeset on one continuous strip of typesetting paper. Make the slots in the posterboard only slightly wider than the paper you will use.

Include in your credits a thank you to everyone who contributed in any way. It is also a good idea to give an address or phone number for feedback and requests for information and copies of the family video. If you created a name for your home "production company," include it with the address and logo. You never know who may end up watching your family video at some future date!

As the last credit passes before the camera, fade to black by using the manual iris if the camera does not have a fade feature. Allow the black to be recorded for approximately five minutes.

Going back to where your credits begin, review the complete segment. You might need a few takes of the credit roll or crawl until you get one in which you are satisfied. This should not be a problem if you left a sufficient tail on the last program visual (The End). When you have a satisfactory credit roll or crawl, including five minutes of black track at the very end, you may now record one last song over the credits. This credit song is really the audio culmination to the production, so give careful thought to choosing a piece which evokes just the right ambiance to conclude the program. There is usually not any narration or other voice during this segment, so the ending song can include vocals. Choose a song which fits the time of the credit roll as closely as possible, having it end as the credits are fading. The song may be cut shorter by fading up the music once it has begun playing, but make sure it sounds natural and not abrupt.

After adding the music to the credits and reviewing it for desired sound, rewind the master tape completely for the final review. It is an exciting moment when the crew gathers to view the completed family video for the first time. When you reach the end, pull the tab on the master tape itself to prevent accidental erasure. The video is now done! All of your hard work is, as they say, "in the can." It may be time for a celebration, but the project is not quite at an end.

Making Copies and Packaging Your Video 5.2

Now that the production of the master tape is finished, you must consider how many copies to make of it. Calculate this by adding up the family list and then make a few more than this total, since families may want two or more copies. You may wish to ask those who want copies to donate a fee per copy to help defray production and tape costs. Another possibility is for family members to make a donation of any amount into a general production fund, and you can give copies of the video upon request.

Great care should be taken to produce the highest quality copies possible of the master tape. Perhaps, if you have sixty hours or more on either machine, it is time to clean your VCR heads again. Use the highest quality videotape affordable for the copies. Although good tape may cost more, everyone will be appreciative years from now that you used it. High quality tape has a much lower dropout rate and a far longer shelf life than the often advertised cheaper tape. We recommend finding a professional video dealer in your area and ordering a case (twenty) or more of professional quality videotape. Often when purchased in this way, it is not much more expensive than buying tape of significantly lesser quality.

By the time you are ready to make copies you should be mostly familiar with different hookups. The equipment and hookups needed for making copies are the same as that of editing option two (see illustration 16, page 68). If you are using an audio mixer or other equipment such as a Hybrid 8, or a similiar switcher/SEG, refer to option three (see illustration 17, page 69). Carefully trace the signal routes of both the audio and video patch cords from the outputs of the slave VCR (which will play the master tape) to the inputs of the master VCR (which will record the copy). As with editing, it is helpful to have a TV/monitor on each VCR.

When all equipment is properly hooked up, you are ready to prepare the copy tape. Fast forward and then rewind each copy tape to adjust them to the master VCR before you begin copying. Make sure the master tape, which has its recording tab removed and is in the slave VCR, is completely rewound. When the copy tape is rewound all the way, both tapes are ready to begin the copying process. Since you will not be editing on the copy and there will be no "breaks" in the audiovisual signals, it is not necessary to lay a black track on each tape.

Set the master VCR on RECORD/PLAY with the PAUSE button down. If you are using an audio mixer, the proper fader bar should be on a middle setting and the master volume control should be on "0." Fade up the master to the proper volume level just before the first audio (possibly the background music) is played by the slave VCR. Then, using the VU meter, make sure that your audio signal being sent to the master VCR remains close to 100 percent modulation, as explained in section 4.1, "A Creative Audio Track."

Next, switch the slave VCR on to PLAY to send the master tape into motion. When it reaches proper speed and the slave TV/monitor shows the black track, release PAUSE on the master VCR to begin recording the copy. Noting the time, calculate when the recording will be completed. Check how the picture looks on the master TV/monitor and if the audio is easy to understand. Fine-tune, as much as possible, the signals which are being sent to the master *before* you begin recording the first copy. When the end of the copying draws near, be ready to fade the audio signal to "0" (if you are using an audio mixer) as soon as the credit song fades away. Let the tapes roll a few more minutes and then place both machines on STOP.

Before you set the VCRs on REWIND *wait a few minutes*. This is important because when videotape is either played or recorded, the process somewhat heats the tape, and warm tape is more likely to stretch when put under the stress of rewinding. Stretching is sure to cause dropouts or other flaws to appear, so wait until the videotape has cooled before rewinding it. The short wait is vital, especially with the master, because any flaws inflicted upon it will be not only repeated but sometimes magnified on each succeeding copy. Since you will want to make multiple copies of the video master, keep it in as new a condition as possible.

When making straight copies, or dubs as they are called, you can spend most of the time doing other things. Once the tapes are allowed to cool and you have rewound them to begin the copying process once again, be sure to check first the ending and then the beginning of each copy to insure that both the audio and visual start and end smoothly. There may be some visual rolling or flickering at the beginning, but this is not serious as long as it does not intrude on the audio track or the first visual. When you are satisfied with the quality of the copy break the tab out of the front edge of the tape cassette, preventing it from being accidently erased. Use these steps to make as many copies as you anticipate the family will want.

You may wish to consider a couple of other very nice finishing touches while you are making the copies of your family video. The first is the type of tape case you may wish to develop. It is possible to purchase videotape cases from good video supply houses which feature a clear sleeve around the outside, allowing the producer to insert a printed cover. A printed case serves as an introduction to the video production and gives the work a professional image even before the tape is put into the VCR. There may be members of the crew who are more comfortable with printed material than with video. For them the design and manufacture of case covers can be the ideal task.

Along with tape covers, another printed item which immensely supports the production is the inclusion into each video case of the complete family tree. An example of this is the photograph in the Introduction. A family tree that viewers may refer to while watching the family video can be a great help to understanding particularly the earlier family generations of the production. Developing the family tree can be a major undertaking, but the results are sure to be worth the effort. Try to have the finished tree fit on sheets of paper which can be included, once folded, inside the tape cases. The family tree is a thoughtful addition to the production, and one which will be appreciated as a companion piece to the video program itself.

There is no better way to celebrate the completion of the family video than to have a "family premiere." Pick a place, date, and time that is convenient and comfortable for a majority of family members. The logistics of such a showing are fairly simple. You will need enough room and seats to accomodate your family members. For a small family perhaps someone's living room will be large enough. For bigger families consider using an empty garage or other large room. Outdoor showings are not advised because it is difficult to position the TV(s) so that the picture is not obliterated by the brightness of the sun. If you are going to form rows of seats raise the TV onto a table to help the view from the back. Use the largest TV obtainable, but it should be one that has a good picture. As always, connect the RF-out of the VCR to the RF (antenna) input of the TV with a coaxial cable (see coaxial cable, in section 4.1, page 45). Once the TV is hooked up to the VCR, check its picture and sound well before show time. You may consider using more than one TV, but if the first set is large, others are usually unnecessary. The seats, formed in a shallow curve in front of the TV, should be adjusted once everyone is seated before you begin the program.

Although the audio systems in TVs are generally improving, they are still usually lacking in a large room setting. Consider connecting the VCR audio-out to an amplifier which can power external speakers. A simple way of doing this is to use a quality portable cassette tape player/recorder, referred to at times as a "boom-box," which is equipped with audio-in jacks. Use a patch cord to connect the audio-out of the VCR to the audio-in jacks of the boom-box, switch the boom box to "source," and play the video soundtrack out of the amplifier's speakers. Using the boom-box or home amplifier allows you not only to control the volume, but also the tone of the audio track, using the bass and treble controls. Boom-boxes are often equipped with graphic equalizers, which can be even more useful in shaping the sound. Consider various audio options, experimenting to find the cleanest sound possible. The degree in which the audio track is successfully comprehendible has a substantial influence on the reaction of the viewers to the production. Keep the volume at levels which allow even the hardest-of-hearing family members to understand without difficulty. Remembering the intensity of the sound track of an action film shown in the theater, try to duplicate that effect with the audio at your family premiere.

The family showing is an appropriate time to return all of the visual materials used to produce the video and also to distribute copies of the video itself to family members. The premiere can evolve into a unique emotional experience as each member is reminded of loved ones and good times from the past. You may wish to designate a special seating section as the "bawling bench" and award the loudest crier the "Golden Kleenex Award." This will add a note of levity to the event, and the thoughtful attention to detail will not be lost by the participants. Depending on the length of the family video, the production crew may each wish to say a few words about their part in making the video. The video may stir old memories which can spark additional "live" family stories all can enjoy following the premier showing.

There will be some family members who cannot attend the family premiere. Mail these people their copies if you are unable to deliver the videos in person. Having lost a number of videotapes over the years through the mail, we would like to add a word of caution. Make sure, if you are using special hard mailing cases for mailing the videos, that the mailing labels are securely attached. Sometimes the labels loosen from the plastic the cases are made from and fall off. So tape the label on with the case shut. An even better method is to use the padded manila envelopes that the post office sells, especially if you are using a printed case cover under the clear sleeve as mentioned earlier. You will not want to mar the outside of the tape case with address labels and other stickers, and the padded envelope protects it from sharp blows in transit. It is also a good idea to insure the tape for a reasonable amount. While this will not guarantee its safe delivery, it will give both you and the post office a record of the transaction.

5.3　Using These Techniques for Other Video Productions

We hope that you can use many of the techniques outlined and explained in this book to enhance future video projects. For example, when again using a video camera for a live shoot, you should remember that a sufficient amount of light makes a significant difference in the quality of the picture. But at least as important, and much easier to forget, is the fact that a video camera cannot tolerate high *contrasts* of light and dark in the picture frame. Bright light is often not as useful in video as one might first think, because it has a tendency to create deep shadows. Establish *even lighting* in the frame, even if it is not as bright as you might like.

Another important feature which distinguishes a quality live shoot from a mediocre one is the type and amount of camera work performed. For instance, it enhances the understanding of the audience to begin each live shoot with an "establishing shot." Then, use the camera angle, zooms, pans, and tilts as tools to emphasize and add meaning to the visual story you are recording with the camera.

Remember what an important part an intelligent audio track plays with good video. If the live audio will remain on the tape, keep the mike as close as possible to the audio source. Since camera mikes are not designed to be hand held, take time to secure the connection on the mike, where the cord plugs in, with tape so there will not be any pops and crackles from movement.

You now know how to add a new soundtrack of either narration, music, or both, to your video productions. Maybe you wish to save the original audio track from a live shoot and add some background music behind it in the editing process. As you videotape, try having the "rock star" of the family lip-sync his or her favorite song. Then use the AUDIO DUB feature on your VCR to record the same song onto the video audio track. If you time the song well you can make a funny family music video to be enjoyed repeatedly. Or maybe Aunt Harriet has played the piano for some years with more determination than accomplishment. The video you have recorded of her begins with the usual rough recital, when suddenly, the song is magically transformed into a professional rendition! It is actually the work of the audio editor, who has dubbed in the professional version by using a record of the same piece.

Another way of enhancing a live shoot is by adding still graphics, especially photos. This simple technique is often overlooked, not only by home enthusiasts, but also by video professionals. Just as a series of photos were used to begin your family video, still graphics introduce a variety of video programs. Another introduction which works nicely is to film the invitation to the event that you are videotaping. Make sure that the invitation can be read with ease on a thirteen inch TV screen.

We will examine in more detail how to apply some of these techniques to three common video subjects: children in general, birthday parties in particular, and wedding ceremonies.

Children

Studies have shown that children are the number one reason that the majority of people buy a video camera. One of the most frequent problems we have seen when videotaping children is that the parents do not take into account the size of their subjects. Often the camera takes a bird's-eye view, producing video footage of a baby crawling on the floor and seemingly pinned to the rug. Filming down on the baby, or any other subject for that matter, is the most repressive camera angle and is to be avoided in almost all cases. Take the camera down near the floor so it is at the *subject's eye level.* Zoom in slowly as the baby crawls toward the camera (and later the viewer). Look at the twinkle in the eye—now that's effective video! Use the same eye-level guideline as the children grow; do not use the camera to "look down" on them as they play in the yard. Children, like adults, look best when they are engaged in a particular activity, so videotape them this way. Try to position the camera so it is involved in the action, as if it was another participant. Use the same eye-level approach when everyone is seated at the table around the birthday cake.

Birthday Parties

With a little forethought you can produce delightful birthday videos to be enjoyed for years. A birthday party is an excellent opportunity to use the printed invitations as the introduction. If the birthday child is more than a year old you can use photos from past birthdays to lead into the live action. Use background music behind the introductory visuals, especially music which is a favorite of the child. Include a few shots of the party preparations and recordings of guests as they arrive are also nice, especially if you can zoom in to your subjects from an inconspicuous location. These are also good establishing shots. Remember to leave a few seconds past the end of each shot so that the next back-roll will not cut off either words or action you want to record. The party itself is easy as long as you keep alert. Be ready to capture each activity, the games, present opening, cake eating, etc. as it unfolds. Mostly you will rely on in-camera editing, so take care to make aesthetically pleasing cuts between segments. While it is always difficult to record live subjects with in-camera edits satisfactorily, with a little planning and discipline you will be able to improve your camera technique appreciably. Try to capture the highlights of the party by striving for quality over quantity.

Weddings

Weddings are obviously a very important event in people's lives, and the videographer should treat them with the appropriate respect. Meet with the prospective bride and her family (or with whoever has requested your services) well before the wedding date. Videotaping weddings is such a new idea that many people, except for wishing the ceremony to be videotaped, are not sure what they want or what they expect. This makes the initial meeting important, allowing you to explain some of the special techniques you plan to employ to make their wedding tape as beautiful as possible. It is also an opportunity to inform the wedding participants what cooperative effort you will need from them to complete your work.

Find out the time and place of the *rehearsal*, and ask permission to attend it. While this request should be easy, the next one is slightly tougher to explain. Tell them you would like to include photographs in the wedding video, particularly photos of the bride and groom when they were babies, and then as they grew, snapshots of them every few years. If there are objections or questions, try to describe how these photos, combined with a lovesong as background music, can become a moving part of the wedding video.

A similar idea is to use the wedding photos of the bride's parents (and earlier generations if available) before the photos of the bride's childhood. The same can also be done for the groom and his family. However, it is often difficult to collect similar photos from both families, so be creative with whatever still material the participants give you. Arrange for the photos to be brought to the rehearsal along with one of the wedding invitations which you may use as an introductory visual. It is essential for you to have the invitation *before* the wedding, but not necessarily the photos.

One other detail to discuss at the meeting is if the bride and groom have a special song or two on record or tape which is especially significant to their relationship. If so, ask them to bring the recording(s) to the rehearsal. If not, suggest a couple of songs befitting a wedding which they might enjoy behind the photos. Almost any love song will do to evoke the proper mood.

At the wedding rehearsal, the first concern upon arriving at the scene of the impending wedding is to determine the best location for the camera. Many videographers and their clients have been content to videotape weddings from the rear of the church or hall. We prefer to place the camera, on its tripod, in the front of the room and off to one side. This way it can face the wedding couple as they stand in front of the officiator. Usually there is a place in the choir section of most churches which works well, and other buildings have even more room in front, so good camera positioning is not a problem. You may have to move some of the flowers, candle stands, etc., on the day of the wedding to have a clear shot of the couple. Use good judgment with these alterations, since some wedding organizers can be apprehensive about such changes in the scenery, however slight. The camera position at the wedding is critical because it is not appropriate to move around at the ceremony, distracting the audience from their proper focus.

Station yourself at the camera location while the rehearsal is in session, taking notes of who enters, where they enter from, and in what succession. This will be important to know on the day of the shoot. Measure the distance to the nearest 110 volt outlet so you will know how long of an extension cord you will need for the ceremony. It is best to save your batteries for the photo session and reception. Remember to collect the photos and invitation.

At home prepare *two* high quality videotapes by fast forwarding and rewinding them with the VCR or camcorder you will use to shoot the wedding. Then, designating one of the tapes to be the master, lay a black track for the length of the tape. Make sure all recording is done on SP mode. When the black track is finished and the tape has cooled, rewind to the beginning. Play fifteen seconds of black and then stop. You are now cued in the proper place to fade up to the invitation placed on your graphics board. You may need to tilt down to get all of the invitation. Record the invitation for about seventy seconds, then stop the camera and rewind, checking the playback. If you are satisfied with how it looks, let the invitation play for about one minute before turning the VCR to

STOP. The master tape is now cued and ready to record the wedding.

On the wedding day, arrive at the site at least an hour before the ceremony so you will have plenty of time to set up your equipment, and also allow for unexpected occurances.

Lighting is often a problem at indoor ceremonies because very few wedding participants are willing to add the lights that video really requires for good resolution. In order not to compound the difficulty, avoid pointing the camera at any bright windows, open doors, or lights when not absolutely necessary. In a darkened interior, this spells glare and washout for the video image.

Another aspect of the wedding shoot which you can control is to record a clean audio track. The goal is to capture the voices of the primary three participants: officiator, bride, and groom. This is almost impossible to do if you leave the mike on the camera; it just will not be close enough to the speakers, and their voices will sound like whispers. The solution to this is to use your mike cord, getting your mike as near to the three subjects as possible. If there are any flowers conveniently near, carefully place the mike among the stems (without getting it wet) and run the cord down the back of the vase. Use tape to keep it in place if necessary. The ideal location is halfway between the wedding couple and the officiator, keeping the microphone perpendicular to the speakers. If there are no flowers in the vicinity, possibly place a green plant somewhere near, hopefully at about waist level, to hold the mike. If this is unavailable, check for other props which might hold the mike in the proper location. Usually there is some way to place the mike near the speakers. Use your creativity to do the best job you can. An understandable audio track is a good enough reason and reward for the effort.

Cue the tape to begin *after* the invitation/introduction finishes, and fade up to record a short segment of the guests arriving. Check your notes from the rehearsal so you know what to expect. Be prepared for all of the important entrances, the parents of the couple, the grandparents, the wedding party, etc., so that the camera will be rolling as they make their way to their places.

The wedding march will cue you to the entrance of the bride, and from that point until the couple's exit, the camera should be left running. Use the zoom to capture a meaningful close-up of the couple as they say their vows but do not over-use camera movements or you will give the proceedings a helter-skelter appearance. For most of the time keep the camera framed at a medium zoom that looks over the officiator's shoulder, with the couple framed from head to knee and the audience slightly out of focus in the background.

After the ceremony, move your video camera so that it has a clear view of the picture-taking session which usually follows. Take a few interesting shots as the participants form into different groups. Then *change videotapes* and continue shooting the photo session a little longer. If you are going to tape some of the wedding reception, use the second tape for it, too. The reason will be explained shortly. At the end of the reception, fade to black at the end of your very last shot on tape two, put the lens cap on, and shoot five more minutes of black.

The day after the wedding you can complete the wedding master, which has the invitation and ceremony recorded on it. Cue it up to a spot in the live photo session that seems appropriate to add the still photos. Set up your graphics board as you did for your family video and prepare for in-camera editing, as shown in illustration 14 (see page 66). Lay out the photos you received at the rehearsal in an understandable sequence. If you know what song you will put behind them, divide the song's total length by the number of photos to find the approximate time each should be recorded. Some may deserve more time than others, so the time you want to add to some must be subtracted from others.

Shoot the visuals as you did for the family shoot. There probably will not be many photos, so the process will not be too time consuming, especially when compared to the family video production. Before adding the background music behind the photos (and invitation at the beginning), use slave to master VCR-editing to add the material recorded on the second tape to the master tape. The photo session is a good place to start adding music, either behind the live audio or in place of it. These sessions do not produce very memorable audio because of the multiple voices. In any event add all of the live segments from the second tape which you intend to use. You may wish to keep just the highlights of the reception, depending on how much tape was shot there and the quality of your in-camera cuts.

Now go back and add the music over the introduction (a solo violin is nice here) and the photo sequence (we usually use a piece such as "We've Only Just Begun," which has been recorded by several artists).

As one final touch, we like to provide the client with three copies of the wedding production: one for the newlywed couple and one for each set of parents. So when you are satisfied with the master, break out the recording tab and make two copies. For one of these copies you can use the second tape from the wedding day, since everything you wanted to use from it has been transferred to the master tape.

One more meeting is necessary to return the invitation, photos, and any musical recordings. You can also deliver the master and two copies of the wedding video. Explain that additional copies are best made from the master, so special care should be taken with it. For videotape this means being stored vertically in a cool, dry place away from direct light and electromagnetic fields, such as produced by electric motors. After playing, they should be allowed to cool before rewinding.

Do not be surprised to receive a phone call before long extolling the fine quality of the wedding video. As you gain more and more experience with video you will develop your own techniques to enhance your efforts.

Glossary

Adaptors (audio/video): Convert one type of audio/video plug, such as a phone plug, into another type, such as a headphone plug.

Attenuator: Matches the input audio signal with the line level of the VCR. It protects the VCR from receiving too strong of an audio signal.

Audio Dub: Records a new audio track on videotape without disturbing the video track (visuals).

Audio Editing: Combines the different sources of audio: narration, music, live speakers, etc., onto the master tape's audio track, thus creating the sound track.

Audio Mixer: Equipment designed to combine audio signals from multiple sources into the single output signal that is recorded as the sound track of a video production.

Audio Track: One of videotape's several tracks (other tracks are control track and video track). VHS format has only one audio track, while Beta has two.

Background Music: Music used behind voices in a video production, which also lends continuity and emotional emphasis to the production.

Back-Roll: The first action a VCR takes when put on PLAY or PLAY/RECORD. This is important to editors using two VCRs because the back-roll time must be calculated when determining editing points.

Cut: The instant, and most common, transition from one shot to another in film or video.

Editing: The adding together of blocks of audio/video material onto videotape to produce a program.

Enhancer: Amplifies the video signal in much the same way an audio amplifier boosts an audio signal.

Fade: A smooth transition, denoting endings and beginnings of segments, whereby the video image either dissolves to black or emerges from black.

Flat Art: Any two dimensional visual material, such as photographs, maps, charts, etc.

Floor Manager: Person responsible for the set and, in particular, the talent during a live shoot.

Fluid Head: A type of tripod head that incorporates fluid in its movement mechanism. Less expensive heads use springs in their mechanisms.

Generation: Video that is transferred from one tape to the next, with each transferral resulting in less resolution. If the master is second generation, copies made from the master will be third, and so on.

In-Camera Editing: The use of a video camera's on/off switch to internally edit visual segments. This method is usually only practical for still graphics.

Input: Jacks by which audio/video equipment receives audio/video signals. Also, the signals themselves (see signal flow).

Jack: An audio/video receptacle which receives a particular type of audio/video plug.

Lighting, Three-Point: Standard triangular studio format lighting with the following three "points."
1. Key light: the main and strongest light.
2. Fill light: eliminates shadows caused by the key light.
3. Back light: located behind the subjects, it adds depth and atmosphere to the set.

Live Shoot: A video recording with live subjects (as opposed to still visuals such as graphics) as the focus.

Master Tape: The production original, it contains every piece of audio/video material and is used to make tape copies.

Master VCR: The VCR which receives audio/video signals in the editing process and records them as the master tape.

Noise: The unwanted sound all audio/video equipment produces. While it can never be eliminated, it should be reduced as much as possible because it degrades the audio/video signals.

On-Line Editing: A type of editing which uses two or more VCRs to record selected tape segments as a video program.

Output: Jacks on audio/video equipment which sends out signals when the machine is activated. Also, the signals themselves (see signal flow).

Pan: Horizontal camera movement right or left (pan right or pan left).

Patch Cord: Shielded cables with audio/video plugs and/or jacks which connect the outputs and inputs of audio/video equipment.

Plug: The male end of a patchcord that fits into the appropriate audio/video jack.

Postproduction: The stage in a video project in which all of the audio/video elements are brought together in the studio to make the master tape.

Proc Amp: A process amplifier stabilizes the video signal. Some proc amps also remove unwanted signal noise.

Production: The stage of a video project that involves live shoots and other video work. Refers to the recording of audio/video information on videotape.

Resolution: A general measure of picture quality used in TV production for video cameras and TV/monitors.

SEG: A special effects generator is a video component which produces various transitional wipes during the program. Used with a switcher it can generate circles, squares, and checkerboard wipes among other effects.

Signal Flow: The route that an audio or visual signal takes, starting from its origin at the output jack, traveling through shaping equipment, and reaching its destination at the input jack of the master or slave VCR.

Slave VCR: The VCR(s) which send audio/video signals in the editing process to the master VCR.

Sound Track: The total of all audio elements used in a media presentation, including narration and music.

SP: Standard Play is the fastest recording/play mode of VHS video. It produces the highest quality recording because the higher speed allows a greater amount of tape surface to pass the head every second.

Storyboard: The record or blueprint from which a video production is built. In addition to listing every piece of audio/video material, it shows camera movement, titles, and every aspect in the post-production of a video program.

Switcher: A video switcher allows the operator to choose from between at least two video sources when selecting an output signal to be recorded by the master VCR.

Talent: Any live subject(s) to be recorded with audio/video equipment.

Tilt: Vertical camera movement up or down (tilt up or tilt down).

White Balance: Feature on a video camera which adjusts the color output by using white as a reference point.

Zoom: Camera lens movement either toward a subject (zoom-in) for a narrower angle of view or away from the subject (zoom-out) for a wider angle of view.

Index

About the Authors

Duane and Pat Sturm are graduates of California State University, Chico (Duane with a B.A. in history, Pat with a B.A. in international relations). Upon graduating the two lived and worked as English teachers in Japan for two years. During that time they worked for Sony Enterprise Company, Ltd., and develpoed an interest in video. After returning to the United States they developed Prismatic Productions, a small format video production business, which focuses on community, family, and documentary video. During 1987, the two organized and produced, with the help of Duane's family, "The Life and Family of Clark and Hanna Sturm." *Video Family History* is the result of experience they gained doing that project and the documentary videos which they have produced. From January 1986 to March 1986, they traveled in a mobile unit throughout Central America (from Northern California to the Panama Canal). From video recorded during that trip, they produced three documentary videos: "Masses and Murals, People and Art of Nicaragua"; "Neighbors Working with Neighbors, International Helping Hands in Nicaragua"; and "The Struggle for Health Care in Nicaragua." In the Spring of 1988, the two produced, "Reclaim the Test Site," a video which documents the largest antinuclear demonstration to date held at the Nevada Nuclear Test Site. All four of these videos are now being distributed internationally.

About the Author